# ways to come home

ALSO BY KATE MATHIESON

*Tea and Travels: Tales of a Nomadic Life*

*Songs of Birds*

# ways to come home

A MEMOIR

KATE MATHIESON

IMPACT PRESS

First published in 2016 by Kate Mathieson
This edition published in 2017 by Impact Press
an imprint of Ventura Press
PO Box 780, Edgecliff NSW 2027 Australia
www.impactpress.com.au

10 9 8 7 6 5 4 3 2 1

Copyright © Kate Mathieson 2016

All rights reserved. No part of this book may be reproduced or transmitted in any form or by any means, electronic or mechanical, including photocopying, recording or by any other information storage retrieval system, without prior permission in writing from the publisher.

'The Lost Hotels of Paris' from REFUSING HEAVEN by Jack Gilbert, copyright © 2005 by Jack Gilbert. Used by permission of Alfred A. Knopf, an imprint of the Knopf Doubleday Publishing Group, a division of Penguin Random House LLC. All rights reserved.

National Library of Australia Cataloguing-in-Publication data:
Author: Mathieson, Kate
Title: Ways to Come Home / by Kate Mathieson
Category: Memoir
ISBN: 978-1-925183-66-5 (print)
ISBN: 978-1-925183-95-5 (ebook)

Cover design: Working Type
Internal design: Brugel Images and Design

The paper in this book is FSC® certified. FSC® promotes environmentally responsible, socially beneficial and economically viable management of the world's forests.

'We need the tonic of wildness.'

Henry David Thoreau, *Walden: Or, life in the woods*

# PROLOGUE

A faded lithograph of a bridge. A smear of peach paint below. One long brush stroke. As if someone made a mistake. Because the rest of the place is as white as fake teeth. White walls. White ceilings.

There are no other pictures in Ward E.

People with pens carry them like scythes. They point them at the sky, emphasising their words, and joust at each other when they disagree. Mostly they scribble furiously and scrawl our stories across paper.

The pen people want to know – *Why? Why? Why?* – and everything is punctuated with this incessant ticking.

Secrets fall out.

When your world falls apart, you can run. Or bunker down, pull across the hatches and squat, hunched but standing, like Atlas. But sometimes, helplessly, you find yourself with nowhere to run and not enough strength to eat a spoonful of old oats floating in milk. And when that happens, when the scaffolding of your life begins to buckle – well, then, *sometimes* ...

You find yourself here.

Where everything is upside down. Your bed, your dreams, your life. You wait by the phone.

But the person who put you here – the one who calls herself your mother – does not call.

**OUTSIDE MY** window a cherry blossom rubs against white shutters. A haze of violet wisteria, thick and round, wraps itself around a wooden gazebo in the park across the street. The smell of spring – new jasmine – wafts gently up to me while in the distance an indigo shroud builds. A sweet storm is coming.

Down below, Parisians stride along the cobbled street. To the boulangerie. To late lunches. To the mysterious places Parisians go. Across the road, a crepe maker takes a break from his hot skillet and lights a cigarette, his feet propped on a milk crate.

*Do I have time for a quick walk by the Seine before the storm comes?* Something tells me I don't as the crepe maker tosses his cigarette into the street and pops up the brown awnings of his shop before he's lost from view. Cafes close. Shutters are drawn. Outside tables are packed away.

Clouds gather. Spring rain lashes, leaving the hot roads steaming. Splatters across my window trying to find a way in. I finger the white envelope. Tickets for tonight. I am excited. Vivaldi. A quartet: two violins, a viola, and my favourite, the cello. Strings, someone once told me, strings have a way of getting inside us. Strings open the heart.

When the kettle clicks I pour a coffee, strong and black. For a while I listen to the rain – on the roof, on the windows, sizzling on the roads below. Finally, I open the royal navy cover of my unlined, uncreased book. Blank cream pages stare at me.

Tomorrow, London. My bag is already packed. A few weeks later, Singapore. Hong Kong. *Is this it? Am I finally going home?*

I write in the middle of the first cream page:

*I am always on the border. Moving – leaving – going to. On the edge of something.*

**IT'S NOT** my first time here.

I've travelled across Europe the past few years, yet I keep returning to Paris. There is something about this city that calls me. Is it the delicious smell of lemons? Of blossoms? The way the light falls, veiling the entire city like a bride of the sun, mysterious and golden?

I first visited three years earlier with a friend, Adrian. He was a seasoned traveller and I was deposited in Europe for the first time.

We rose with the midday sun, strolled down alleyways without maps and ate our way through Paris. I had never eaten so much. While I showered in the small hotel bathroom, Adrian selected fresh baguettes and wheels of impossibly soft cheese that seemed to spill onto my bread and spread themselves. The takeaway coffee was perfect, strong and sweet, but strangely served in thin white cups (water cooler ones) that burnt through the plastic and scalded my fingertips.

We sauntered up and down the Seine, crunching over gravel. Cherry blossom petals scattered in the breeze, a flushed carpet for us to tread upon.

I awoke from a mid-afternoon nap to find Adrian standing in our hotel room with two strong lattes (double cupped) and an assortment of French patisserie bites. Morning delights.

A sense of freedom emerged. I could do anything today – I could stay in bed if I wanted; drive to Berlin; take the overnight train through Switzerland. I could, I could, I could …

Possibility became a drug. Bold and innocent, I felt it could lead me anywhere.

So I let it.

**IN THE** heat of that first European summer I found myself moving north to Edinburgh. Summer, strong and sunny, did not last for long. It burst in full bloom as I arrived, then retreated just as quickly. There was a sharp month of autumn when leaves turned crimson and shed into piles knee-deep. Winter quickly closed in. Grey clouds gathered, and snow began to fall.

I started a casual job at the local hospital, secretary to a professor of surgery. The days were enjoyably silent, patients slept and doctors prepped for operations. Mostly I typed, answered an occasional phone call. At times the only sounds I heard in hours were the whir of the kettle and the nurses' soft shoes, whispering down the hallway.

The city slumbered all those months. The sky smudged through three simple transitions – pitch night blackness; the silver translucence of dawn; and sometimes, for a few hours, the eerie light of ashy day.

As winter deepened, the city became a place of eternal night. Stars hung close to the earth. Snow fell, lightly at first, landing silently on the ground. Fresh layers of powder sat waiting each morning, white and new. Up at dawn, I made the first mark with giant snow boots that squeaked while the rest of the city slept.

Navigating the streets was an art form I had to learn quickly: avoid the sludgy snow with tyre marks. Take care of the black ice, hidden like secrets, treacherous and slippery. Many times I fell heavily, before learning to throw salt on the pavement to wear away the ice. Bruised elbows. Puffy knees. Jarred ankles.

I tied a scarf around my face lest the breeze slice at my cheeks like razor blades. Step delicately, carefully through drizzle; more rain; sleet; snow. At times, Scotland's squall had enough force to push you back where you came from. I learnt to walk against the felling wind, like a hunched granny with weakened bones, cleaved at the middle, head first.

When the cold began to seep too far into my bones (three months without sun), I flew to Cyprus. I peeled off trench coats and woollen jumpers and threw my pale veined body at the feet of the ocean, like a gift at an altar, worshipping the sun. I had colour again. Remembered the feeling of bare arms. The smell of sea salt. The tang of lemons on fish.

I stayed for a week longer, then two, before the Mediterranean breezes pushed me north …

**PASSIONATE AND** eager, the Greeks were impossible not to like. Food the currency of their love, I sat at blue-and-white checkered tables eager to eat after months of stodgy Scottish fare. Robust tomatoes split easily, leaking seeds and sweet juice. Terracotta dishes filled with hard black olives made my hands greasy and when no-one was looking, I licked them clean. Tzatziki made from home-grown cucumbers scattered with handfuls of ripped mint. I piled spoonfuls onto large plates of flat bread, larger than my face, and rolled them up like a kebab, eating them quickly, dipping the ends into plates of salt and oil.

It became a delicious way to avoid the bustling hot streets. I slipped into these kafeneía often, when the midday sun scorched the earth and my arms threatened to burn. Outside, fuchsia bougainvillea grew wildly between the stone walls; places people told you they never could.

On Sundays, by the port, market stalls popped up, a small town of white plastic tents. Farmers sold crates of snake beans and large heads of leafy lettuce from the back of their vans. Mint and rocket wore damp soil on their roots, fresh from the fields that morning.

I strolled back and forth, tasting olives and fried zucchini flowers, buying homemade almond butters and green beans, and watching the fishermen cast nets into the ocean from small dinghies. Slabs of feta, sold by the brick at the corner of the marketplace, tempted me every time. I always bought more than I could eat. Wrapped in a light paper to take home, I'd cut generous pieces, like I was slicing a cake, and eat the salty slivers on their own.

There was a lovely sense of my body resetting, my skin shedding its dry, scaly cover. My right hip, which had ached all Scottish winter, suddenly seemed oiled and happy. A feeling of restoration and rejuvenation came over me. One that can only come with connection to the outdoors, eating things from the earth, and of course with time. I had time for everything. Time to talk. Time to listen. Time to meander. Time to eat. Time to breathe. Time to sleep, and sleep well.

Things I had never noticed before started to make themselves known. The way the sea smelt differently from morning to evening. The soft yellow undercarriage of a pelican's beak. The feel of my wooden front door after a full day in the sun. The smell of fresh fish frying in lemon and salt. The sound of bees blown by the afternoon breeze. This way of life worked like a meditation, slowing down time. Even – possibly – winding it back.

'You do not need to know precisely what is happening,' wrote the French poet and mystic Thomas Merton, 'or exactly where it is all going.'

*Where is the magic in that?*

I found myself boarding a plane, then ferry, headed for Croatia. Dubrovnik was a city to be wandered, offering gifts to those who sauntered. Old houses one on top of another, neapolitan shutters; strawberry, chocolate and vanilla.

Crumbled walls marked every part of the city. Shells and bullets from the war had penetrated to the core, but a decade on plants grew through the gaps – winter oilseed rape and caper plants and soft green ferns. Spaces could always be filled. Even the weeds with buttery heads were beautiful.

It was a hard city to leave, as was Rome, and Riga and Innsbruck, and all the places that came after.

I came to love them all; these places that shaped me.

**WHEN I** think about the shape of me, more clearly than anything else I see Jason. Dark hair with a fringe cowlick. Skin the colour of milk. Arms that wrapped around me, and fastened, like a seatbelt. Never letting go, even when it felt like we were crashing.

After many years together, we had begun, like wood, to curve and bend in the same places. Even being separated by oceans and continents for the last few years could not undo the shape of us – or so I thought.

But he had grown exhausted by my need to seek, to be elsewhere. My pleas for 'just another few months' over a crackling phone line were met with silence. Not believing it was the end of our relationship, I refused to return to Australia and continued to explore the world. Our worlds trundled along; we allowed months, a year to go past without talking. We were together. And we were not.

By the summer of 2005, sitting in this Parisian hotel watching the French women walk to boulangeries, and late lunches, waiting for the storm to pass, I call him for the first time this year. He speaks for fifteen minutes about the weather, his job, before asking, 'Where are you?'

I have to say Paris three times.

Finally, he takes a deep breath and says, 'I'm engaged.'

I forget to breathe. To taste. I forget I have legs and am sitting in this blue-backed wing chair. I forget how lovely the rain sounds on the window.

I ask in a tight voice, 'Are you happy?'

'I think so,' he says. And I know it is only for me, to soften the blow.

She is everything I am not: steady; homemaker; child-bearer.

I say I have to be somewhere, and hang up the phone.

But I don't.

I leave the hotel room and go out into the pouring rain, walking blindly towards the Seine. The crepe man has closed up and gone home. The streets are empty. People shelter inside cafes and restaurants. Large gusts of wind whip the flower heads off the wisteria, scattering them across the ground. They stick to my shoes, and make a purple paste.

My clothes seep with rain and cold. The air is slightly smoky – fireplaces have been lit. Blankets pulled out. Winter is not over yet. My lungs grow tight. Something else is seeping into me too – regret. *Have I stayed away too long?*

Perhaps. It is hard not to think about my friends in varying stages of stability, engaged and happily married. Living in large houses on the edge of the city. Mortgages. Job promotions. Some with baby number two or three sleeping deeply in small, hand-painted cribs.

I walk past a closed restaurant; a church with stained windows; Mary's hands holding a small, soft body towards the light, a sweet smile of grace; a fountain overfilling, a million teardrops clinging to the sandstone sides, before spilling onto the ground. I am not convinced but I think of this other life, this blissfully domestic, safe and stable life. *Do I want those things?*

**I'D SPENT** my childhood besotted with snow globes of cities. Copenhagen. Wellington. New York. London. I thought it amazing that a whole city could fit into my palm. Turning them upside down, shaking the snow around, and then upright, the beauty of silence and the glitter flakes falling to the ground. I looked for tiny people against the city skyline. If you stared hard enough, you could spot them floating about in the jelly water that filled each globe, bobbing down the street, forever frozen in the city.

I had proudly lined them up, those snow globes, on my mantelpiece, and thought, *This is what I'll do when I'm older, when I grow up, I'll line things up on my mantelpiece.* Except instead of snow globes, there would be vases of flowers, and glazed pottery jars. And a kitchen of cast iron skillets and roasting pans where I'd cook delicious Sunday lunches for hours.

I wonder if Jason's kitchen has glazed pottery jars. Would they roast chickens? Or roll eggs into flour and make fresh fettucine? Would they listen to opera and pour glasses of shiraz as they smile at each other, barefoot on the wooden floor?

The rain eases. The wind blows from the south, warmer. I can smell again the slight honey sap of spring in the air. I buy a coffee from a small corner shop. I walk over the trash that has collected in the streets. I pull the leaves from my hair. There are a thousand flowers drowning in the fountains. Above me the sky is a square of silver, as if any moment the sky might send more rain.

On the street beside me, a woman struggles putting a puffy jacket on her child, who is refusing to be covered. Something in my heart flares. Stop resisting. Give in.

I go inside the hotel. And book a ticket home.

**SYDNEY IS** just as I had left her – glary and loud. From the time I exit the airport, buses are wheezing and braking. Phones are ringing. Loud conversations. Chatter on quiet carriages. Ads shouting from underground train screens. People on microphones inviting me to shop. To eat. Korean bbq. Peking duck. Creamy coffee. Chocolate croissant. Butter popcorn. Grilled burgers. Bread by the roll. Bread by the loaf. Make it healthy. Sushi. Salad. Smoothies. Green juices – someone's saying, 'Gotta eat healthy.' Join Us – gyms – free two-week passes. Medicare – Medibank – HCF – 'Now's the time'. Banners – posters – bus signs. MasterChef – Kitchen Rules – restaurant renovations. Appointments – dentists – doctors. Sell – buy – lights – vacuums – dusty computers. Never have enough – cafes – cinemas – clubs. Pumping music so the bass breaks through the pavement beneath our feet.

I pretend then, blanketed by noise and striding with the crowd, that surely, I must be full. And isn't full another word for happiness?

But, of course, it isn't.

Yet I am convinced I can make it work. I rent houses, cottages by the beach. Units in the city centre. Townhouses in the trendy inner west. Each time picking something that isn't quite right – too noisy, too quiet, too close to things, too far from things, isolating, suffocating.

I buy suits and high heels. Take jobs like you might embark on a love affair: with a swift novelty and an upward crescendo before they descend into monotony and stutter bleakly past their use-by dates.

I rise at five in the morning to run the vacuum over the carpet that seems to dirty every day. I leave the house without make-up and spend the long train ride elbow to elbow with weary commuters. Emails and endless cups of black coffee fill the hours. The fluorescent lights above our cubicles flicker occasionally but never tell us the real time of day.

The midday city streets smell of petrol and fumes and hold too many people. They are shoved into buses, queued out of stores and crammed onto streets – into me. They are close enough that I can smell their stale cigarette breath, and their earthy ripe sweat under heavy wool suits.

Their thoughts seem to seep out of their pores too – the angry, the sad, the depressed, the stuck – and hang in the air like mist. If you are unlucky enough to pass, in the next few seconds, you'll be covered by it too.

The sprees of sun do little to soothe me, and the wind keeps roaring through the streets, sending everyone off balance.

At dusk, I join commuters jostling in lines for crammed buses and trains that stop at every station, taking over an hour to find mine. I am always home after dark, where I make dinner quickly and spend the rest of the night listening to the TV as I wash the dishes, elbows deep in suds. Too tired to read, I lie in bed watching the ceiling and listening to the far-off sounds of cars on the motorway, my alarm set for 5 am.

After months of this churning, I can't tell whose thoughts I am bringing home when I worry about money, or bills, or the list of chores I have to do. On the weekend, I am too exhausted to do anything but sleep away the thoughts.

Family and friends smile at me over coffee. 'You've finally settled down.' Relieved comfort in their voices. 'You used to be so wild. So crazy.'

They cluck and natter and laugh, as if I had been off piste and they had made every effort to bring me back.

'So, are you going to buy a house now? Find a husband?'

I try to imagine the life they paint for me. It means sharing my tiny bathroom, trying to decide if we need two cars or one, the stress of deciding what to have for dinner, who gets to shower first as we both run late for the train. There would be double the amount of plates to wash at night.

On weekends we would tell ourselves we need to be independent. He'd golf. Or drink beer with his friends and stay out later than I liked. I'd go to yoga, and have coffee with the girls and then fret whether I should make the vegetable pie or lasagna for our dinner party and how many bottles of white to buy, which candles to put out?

On Sunday we'd end up staring at the million tints of paint at the hardware store struggling to find the perfect match for the bedroom walls whose shade never pleases us. We'd never get around to fixing the garage eaves that continue to rot before our eyes from the inside out.

**DAYS OF** to-do lists. Days of picking up dry cleaning, and three-hour meetings. Days of rushing to the supermarket for Nurofen or baby spinach leaves that haven't wilted to mush, laying in my crisper too long. World Cup fever hits Sydney. Everywhere is offering jugs of beer and bowls of wedges and giant television screens are erected so we can cheer on Australia. There are words you cannot say as an Australian: I don't like sport. I don't watch rugby. I didn't realise there was a game. But there is the offer of wine – the chance to see friends. In front of the giant televisions, we uncork champagne, give cheek kisses, hugs, talk about the weather. Our jobs. Their kids.

There is the announcement of a new baby girl. Drink. A celebration of ten years married. Drink. Someone has a new million-dollar mortgage, a small townhouse with a square of cement that is close to 'good schools'. Drink. The champagne has run out. I queue at the bar, for what feels like hours, to order two more bottles. Standing in line, with the World Cup blaring in the background, I meet a man who is a sales trainer. Travels for work. No two days are the same. A man who seems just as mercurial as me. He slips me his number, and then thinks better of it. Asks for mine, and promises to call.

He calls.

We spend weekends finding good coffee. Strolling through markets. Afternoons comparing bikes, planning trips, choosing mountains to hike, finding museums to stroll through. He, from country stock, makes a garden bed for me out the back of my unit. Wood-panelled and high-rise. His large, earthy hands so assured. I wait with cucumber seeds to sow. Within a month, we are picking the small slender fingers. They don't need anything – we could eat them alone – but we pour olive oil and salt on top and let them marinate. A month later, we have baby tomatoes that are full of sunshine, large-leafed basil, Italian mint and thyme and oregano too.

I remember how it feels to be close to someone: how delicate it is to fit into the grooves of their body, learning how their neck smells, knowing whose thumb will be on top when you hold hands, how they like their eggs, the way my heart pounds when they make a perfect morning coffee – black and strong and bitter – with a side pot of real cream. I think I know what our future looks like: walking around Paris in the rain at 2 am, taking a small leaky boat to an off-cut island, tucking inside ourselves, lying next to each other, reading books at night with our big toes touching. Everyone has another world, under their noisy world, that lays mostly forgotten. This is mine.

**WE MOVE** into a cold, ground floor flat, two train stops from the Sydney Harbour Bridge. Our lives settle into the city rhythm. Work, Monday to Friday. At night I cook and he watches *Ice Truckers*. Sometimes he cooks and I watch re-runs of *Friends*, but early on he makes a pasta sauce with a bottle of rogan josh and some baked beans and too much salt, so we laugh and order pizza and decide he shouldn't be allowed near the kitchen again.

Life is: glasses of shiraz and a slab of brie, then shower-scum fighters and half price carrots, Sunday morning cafe big breakfasts – eggs, thick-cut white toast, lashings of butter, a side of grilled tomatoes. Extra avocado.

Under the Harbour Bridge, we drink cups of hot chocolate from a French cafe, where we melt dark chips above a tea-light candle, in a small ceramic dish. Add splashes of full cream milk, stir it together, thick as honey, then sip it through a metal straw. He flies me to Melbourne, where we walk hand in hand around the wintery city, scarves and coats, gloves and boots, the sun a tiny pea-sized drop, doing little to warm the stone buildings. Here, we swallow as much art and coffee as the weekend will fit.

In Federation Square, I get a phone call – an old friend is engaged. She can't wait for us to return. I put her on speakerphone. She is exuberant.

Can you believe it? We all keep saying. Congratulations. Her partner is laughing; he hid the ring in a box for weeks. Booked a hatted restaurant. A luxury suite. Wore a tux and got down on one knee. Champagne. Roses.

Do you want that too? He asks later.

I blink. I'm not sure if he is joking. It is a good thing that it begins to rain then, large fat, splatting rain. We dash for the first open door we can find. A church. Inside everyone is shivering and laughing, the gathering crowd presses in. Umbrellas are shaken. Coats appear from bags. Someone mops their head with a newspaper. I watch puddles of water grow large on slippery tiles. Someone keeps asking, 'Has it stopped?'

At the airport, he holds my hand the whole flight, orders me a wine and another – knowing I can't stand the feeling of whizzing through the air in a metal bird. The strangeness of it. I clutch the seat edge every time the engines switch gears. Someone's light dings, because they want extra water. A blanket. I imagine a million things I'd never say: a fireball igniting the wings. Another plane flying into us. The engines giving up completely, everyone clawing at each other to get to the exits, the lights flickering and a dark descent into the open mouth of the ocean, before sinking to the very bottom. Would we die on impact? These are the thoughts that I have, while I am drinking a pinot noir and not tasting it. While I am peeling back the plastic on my cheddar cheese and crackers. I do not breathe properly until the Airbus wheels hit Sydney tarmac.

When we get home, I unpack and he orders butter chicken and extra rice. Garlic naan. Pappadums. He lays out a blanket on our chocolate suede couch, tucks us both into it.

I think, *I should be happy.*

**THE SLOW,** cold Saturdays entice me to stay in bed. I hear him shower and change and unlock the bike. I lie under the blankets for hours. I listen to the clock in the kitchen. To a fly that can't find its way out of my living room as it hovers and hits the window, its wings beating against the glass. Ten feet above me, our neighbours start yelling. Someone next door is moving furniture, like giants shoving steel bookcases against our wall.

I open the window an inch and try to shoo it out, but even though there is an exit, an escape, the fly stays where it is. I watch as it becomes quiet in the corner of the wood, then lies there defeated. I shower.

When I check an hour later, it has died. I cup the body in both hands and toss it gently out the open window, to the place it had been trying to find. The silence, marked only by the kitchen clock, grows like moss and vines, and fills each room. If I stay inside any longer, I'll go mad.

I grab my keys and leave. Jeans and a loose t-shirt are not a smart choice in winter, but at least the chill makes me feel alive. For a second I breathe in the smog from the city, the smell of trees from the morning rain. I listen to the buses rattle up our street. I walk to the shops. Then find myself on a train, going north.

There are a group of older women who have been lunching in the city. They smell of heavy musk perfume and sauvignon blanc. A middle-aged couple discuss a job promotion in Singapore. Two teenage girls swap gold and black nail polish. I listen to their conversations – stock markets, weather, to tennis or not on Saturday, wines to try, silk tops to buy, who is dating, divorcing, desperate.

The train terminates at the end of the line. Hornsby. I think about continuing on to Newcastle, further up the east coast of NSW, and beyond. I think about not going in to work on Monday. I think about taking the train to the airport, and getting on the next flight.

But I don't go anywhere. I sit on the empty platform with a bitter takeaway coffee warming my hands.

In the end, I get on a train towards our flat. The whole way back, I stare out the window at the world, as if through a telescope at stars.

At home I find myself staring into a malnourished fridge. An old rind of cheese. His JD and coke cans. Wilted lettuce. Old broccoli. Pasta from a few nights ago. I lift the lid, looking for the white fungus that always gathers when we leave things too long.

When he gets home at 7 pm he declares he is starving. So I scrape the white fungus off the pasta, reheat it and served it on a white plate and tell myself it doesn't matter what he doesn't know.

**THE WINTER** rain becomes incessant. It doesn't give up for a full fortnight – gutters overflow. Shoes are soaked. Everything feels damp inside our flat, under our blankets. My pillow smells slightly of mildew. Our ceiling comes out in spots, and on further inspection while on a ladder, he determines the diagnosis: black mould. We purchase extra heaters for around the house. Plug gaps in our windows. We relent and buy a dryer – it's either that or new clothes. Stock up on carpet doorstops to keep the rain and winter breath from finding a way inside.

Everything feels distant; we talk about a holiday to America but don't book anything. We disagree on small things: how the sheets should be folded, how much to spend on birthday presents, whether we should drive four hours to see his parents for the weekend, which route to take, what songs to listen to.

We do laundry. Eat roast potatoes. I remember to buy biscuits when we are low. He sticks bills on the fridge with a little red magnet. We wash sheets and hang them out, and bring them in and fold them silently.

I think secretly about standing on the roof one night and letting them go into the wind. Where would they land?

I resign from my government communications job and take a corporate offer. He gets a promotion. We have more money and less time.

We buy things we do not need: better shirts, designer pants, nicer bottles of wine. I spend nights scrolling through work emails that people send at 10 pm, 11 pm, midnight, each accompanied with the red-hot poker of an exclamation point: high importance.

I try to not want this life, but I watch my bank balance double. I think about all the places we can go. Six months in a French chalet. A villa in Tuscany. Watching the aurora borealis from an igloo.

Rather than feel comforted, I am somehow disappointed. It is the feeling I get when the alarm goes off at five. When I have to stay late at work. When I can't seem to balance myself. It is the feeling of lethargy and decline, the kind that you feel when someone forgets your birthday, makes plans and doesn't turn up, says they like you – then never calls.

More rain. I unpack my old boots I brought home from London. We waterproof our jackets. The toaster breaks. On Sunday he takes it apart, bit by bit. Fiddling with screwdrivers. Sighing into the grates. He fixes it, but leaves it with a limp. It will not balance anymore on our white kitchen countertop. I get annoyed every time I plunge a piece of bread into the gap, that I have to hold the toaster, otherwise it will tip. He keeps saying, I don't know why it's doing that; I'll take another look at it.

Then, just when I least need it: Jason emails. I am sitting at my desk between meetings. The phone is blinking at me – eight missed calls. Messages lined up. My inbox shows forty-eight unread emails. And then forty-nine – his name appearing at the top. It is short and perfunctory. *Hello*. He does not address me, and I wonder if this is a group email, something he has copied and pasted and sent to everyone. My eyes catch on the words below. *We are having a baby*. My stomach twists. I feel dizzy. Is it the baby that disturbs me? Or the notion of a 'we'?

I delete it without reading the rest. I grab my coat and bag. Leave work without telling anyone. On the way home I watch my pale, startled face reflected in the grubby train window. I go to bed at 3 pm, still wearing my white silk blouse. I cry into my pillow.

I worry that I have come back for nothing. That I have given everything up.

I worry about worrying.

He creeps in later, thinking I am asleep, and slowly slides between the sheets. He snores. I watch the stars. The moon moves across the window.

*I hope I can pull myself out of this.*

Me too, I say aloud.

**WHEN MY** birthday arrives, I don't feel like celebrating. *What have I done this past year?* I want to stay in bed, but we drive to the Blue Mountains – a place of fir trees and cliff winds and knee-high piles of leaves. We eat dinner at a lovely restaurant – cheese and leek tarts, hand selected spinach and baby peas bathe in oil and parmesan. Before dessert, the chef takes us outside and points out the organic garden. We walk through it. Spinach grows up woven wire, waving in the wind and tickling our shoulders. New potatoes glow like moons in the ground. We share a lemon pie for dessert and lick our spoons clean. The coffee is locally ground – strong and black, exactly as I like it.

At night, when he snores, I go outside and listen to the wind come up the valley, roaring like a wave. I almost feel normal again.

Just before midnight, I fall asleep and have a series of consecutive nightmares; I am trapped at the bottom of the sea, drowning. A plane is burning and crashing. I am stuck in cement and birds are pecking at my hair, my eyes, whilst a red wind screams through the world.

I wake shivering. My head pounds. I am hot and then cold. I can't get out of bed. He wraps me up in a bathrobe, as though he is scared if I touch anything I'll break.

It's just a cold, he says, searching through our toiletries for Panadol, Nurofen and cough elixir.

Is it? I lay in the bed, shivering below blankets, staring glumly at the ceiling. It is hard not to think of Paris. Of Greece. The sun lighting trees ablaze, a row of pines bending in late summer winds. The smell of salt on my skin. How all of it tasted like freedom.

What is the difference, I wonder, between people who grow deep roots into the soil, and the ones who ride the wind with outstretched wings? Could curiosity be just another way of bravely living?

In the afternoon, I sleep fitfully. After sunset, he brings my birthday to me – champagne and a berry tartelette. When I cut a slice, the berries bleed onto the knife. The knife chinks against the porcelain plate. My present is wrapped tight and well. A million bits of sticky tape to get through. A black wool jumper with a high neck. Wear it to dinner, he suggests. When I try it on, the wool tightens around my throat and scratches my skin.

I feel an immediate panic. My heart forgets to beat. I pause, but can't hear it. My lungs aren't moving. Nothing is going in my nose.

*I can't breathe*, I think frantically.

Oh. Dear. God.

*I CAN'T BREATHE.*

I lunge for the lamp and turn it on. Only when the light spills across the room do I finally take a big, wheezing gasp.

'What's wrong?'

'I can't breathe.'

'If you can talk, you can breathe.'

I watch a spot then, on the carpet. Bite my lip. Wait. Make sure I can breathe, not just voluntarily, but that my brain can manage the involuntary notion of breathing while I am doing other things. Like sleeping. Eating.

I count. Six inhales. Six exhales. Seven. Eight.

'Can you turn out the light now? Can we go to dinner?'

*There's something wrong*, I think. I am too young to be having trouble *breathing*.

The restaurant is empty when we arrive. I don't remember ordering risotto with tiny peas. Eating it. Drinking a glass of wine that could have been water. Later we put on coats. Scarves. Gloves. We take a walk. Leaves whip around us. I think the birds must have gone to sleep, roosted for the night. But if I look closely, there they are, wing tips, night flying, their eyes capturing the moon, gleaming.

When we get back I sit on the edge of the bath, staring at the white walls. I know I should go back out, but I don't. I stay listening to myself, breathing, until he knocks on the door.

I run the bath and pretend to get into it. I make fluttery watery sounds every now and then, skimming my hands across the cooling water. I watch the walls. Stare at my pale reflection in the mirror. An hour later it sinks in: we don't need to keep going. Keep struggling. Keep at something that isn't meant to be kept.

I get up and leave the bathroom, grab chocolate and a book and curl up in my bed and think, *FUCK*. Am I here again? Am I failing? Why can't I seem to get it sorted? Why do I keep falling into places I shouldn't be?

In the quiet, he comes into the bedroom, holding a tea. It smells like soft fruit flowers. He leans over, brushes his fingertips against my forehead, like he is a nurse checking for fever. With the blankets pulled tight below my chin, swallowing my body, I am just a head stretched on a bed – thinking too much. I say the words I have needed to say for a while, 'It's over.' He looks away for a while, then back at me, nods slightly. He finishes his tea, turns on the news. A bomb in Iraq has killed sixty. He carefully folds his clothes into his suitcase and takes it out to the car.

I don't sleep that night. I walk to the edge of the woods in a coat that does little to warm me. The trees spread out gnarled roots, and in most places, the last autumn leaves have given up and fallen. As I walk, my world becomes a leafy canvas, dark and damp and cold.

I thought I would feel happy, casting myself off like a ship into the night bound for any port, to go where the tide wishes to carry me, but I don't.

I feel lost and loose and without an anchor.

**I MOVE** to a small white house near the woods on the far edge of the city.

Because I have a house, with a fully fenced yard, it quickly follows that I need a gardener or a crash course in mowing my lawn (and a mower), and because my nine-to-five is really a 7 am to 8 pm I get a cheap fortnightly cleaner too. All these things neatly file themselves under the title, Responsibilities. And I, now with many of them, feel quite entrenched in this little spot I have chosen as mine.

Spring rinses the city with honey sap. I take a running leap back into life: I begin French lessons. Cello lessons. I learn how to make milk chocolate on long marble benches. I stand around a local hall in the evenings, trying to master the sway of salsa and samba.

Our suburb is awash with wattle. It tickles my nose and brings the burring of bees. I buy seasonal lemons from the farmers market, the shape of eyes, and they sit in my kitchen and watch me intently as I make sugary lemon crepes and pretend I'm in France.

I plant chamomile and think about the best time to pick the baby buds, steeping them for tea. Lemon balm grows rapidly like a weed, but I can't get the coriander to hold. The bugs enjoy the basil as much as I do. Luckily there is enough for both of us; it grows to my hip within a month. The soil must be fertile here.

## ways to come home

An elderly gentleman down the street tells me my house has been with the same family owners for almost a century, that in the 1940s they used the backyard to grow their vegetables and fruits – they never needed to attend the local shops, except for cuts of sirloin and brisket. The original owners raised four children there, and only moved out in the eighties when the husband died peacefully in his sleep.

All this land around me, the woods, the fertile soil, the sound of kookaburras in the morning, the peaceful wash of breeze through leaves in the evening. But still, at night, I can't sleep. I rely on naps; in the train, dozing in the night, but most of the time I spend awake. After a month, my life is too much to keep up; I quit French. I stop making chocolate. I let the samba steps slide from my mind. I zip up my cello and place her in the garage, promising to return. I don't.

I continue to go to work. Write emails. Approve plans. Come home.

I must wait until I have done a full 8.5-hour day before I can swipe my card and leave the building. They clock us in and out. Our breaks too. There is an entire team, somewhere in another building, watching to see we complete our hours each week. It has a 1984 Orwellian ring to it. Some days, with little work to do, I sit there, knowing I can't leave. Having looked up the internet on anything I'd ever wanted to know: the Latin word for hedgehog, the best coffee in my suburb, the world's weirdest burger, the most popular boys name, the percentage of people who hate their job (66 per cent), I drink too much coffee, then overload on water in a bid to balance it, then spend the afternoon asking if I can please leave a long three-hour meeting to use the bathroom – again.

There is no prison like the one you willingly walk into every day.

It sours my sleep, presses into every thought, makes me feel I am locked in a chest, thrown off a cliff into the ocean. Sinking – but still with an air pocket.

I try to rekindle my life. New books. A drive to the beach. Watching French films at a local festival. I buy an orange tree, mature and budding with fruit, and stand it at my door. Now every time the wind blows, I smell blushing blood blossoms and the cleanliness of citrus.

But no matter what I do, each day feels fixed, the same as before.

I buy things I don't need. An Italian suit. Tiffany earrings. A new sofa.

**THE TRUTH** reveals herself. I don't want those things on the mantelpiece after all. A life lined up. I want to walk for days along the glaciers of Norway without seeing anyone, or swim off Cape Tribulation as far as I can. I want the rush of Icelandic wind against my cheeks, the smell of pine trees, to walk barefoot among the wild woods where wolves sleep.

I begin to notice how everything out there, in the wild, seems to move. Oceans. Sharks. Wolves. Elephants. Rivers. Nothing stays in the same place. I want to be like them too, to keep moving.

People look at me as if I am absurd. *You have to have a place, some where you can stay, settle down. Don't you?* It isn't a question.

I am, to the people that stay easily in one place, lacking something they hold in bountiful amounts – resilience, fortitude, maturity. They have been taught that life was about staying put, working hard, sticking it out, being strong.

Friends look at me strangely. *You want to just leave? Again?* They laugh. *Where will you live? How will you earn money?*

I can't answer, so think it best to make a plan. If not to follow it, then at least to have something to tell others about. Each weekend – in-between vacuuming the living room and tugging old clumps of hair from my shower drain – I try to conjure one.

I sit with a blank sheet of paper in front of me. At the top I write, *Plan*, but underneath I can't scrawl anything. I think perhaps it would work better if I list things, point by point, of what I should do.

So I write the number one and then a full stop. And below it, two, and another full stop. But even this precursor can't elicit any words to join their numeric counterparts. Soon the page just becomes a series of numbers, like I am practising counting, and by the end I have reached one hundred – Norway and Iceland feel very far away.

*I should just leave*, I think. Pack my bags. Go.

I open up my suitcase. I throw in a book. A pair of old jeans. *Where exactly am I going?* I sit down on the edge of my bed. Beyond the window, clouds gather, the smell of rain coming. A spider in the corner of my house spins a lacy web.

Mostly, this is as far as I get.

**A KIND** of madness settles within me. It comes long after the exhaustion and a brief but unrelenting shroud that some might call depression. The madness has a quirk to it. I'm not yelling at strangers or forgetting to wear clothes. I'm not cuffed and sectioned by the police, or squatting in the corridor of a hospital, peeing through my jeans and underwear. (I had once seen a woman in mid-psychosis do exactly this.)

No, my madness is noticeable only to me, and that is a dangerous thing.

I struggle to remember words. On occasion I forget my own name. I begin to forget why I am getting up in the morning – *What is the point of it all?* – so I sleep later. I lose my brush and never buy another one, so my hair begins to curl and tangle. One night I wake with pins and needles in my left side that won't subside. Quickly afterwards, I lose the feeling in my left leg too. When I start seeing sparks of light like a camera flash in my eyes minutes later, I call the local health line.

'Lay down. Right now.'

'Why?' I ask, feeling my voice rising to a weird high-pitched screech. 'What's wrong with me?'

'We think you're having a stroke. Lay down.'

I do as they ask: I open the front door, hang up the phone, lie down in the hallway and wait. From across the other side of the train line I hear faint ambulance sirens wailing their way towards me.

At the hospital nurses bustle around me, connecting me to cords and wires. Doctors ask me a series of questions.

'Have you been away recently? Overseas?'

My mind is blank. *I don't know.*

'Have you been in any rivers?'

*I don't know.*

'Have you had a fever?'

*I don't know.*

There are a series of tests. Walk straight. Hold one knee up. Hold the other knee up. Hold a pen. Write. My right side is complicit, performing all tasks admirably well. My left side is numb and slow. I keep opening and closing my left fingers, and even though my eyes say I should feel something, I feel nothing. It is a hand that belongs to someone else.

There is a CT scan. An MRI. Multiple blood tests. The doctor makes several hushed phone calls, mentioning words like neurological disorder, quick onset, unstable and stress. And all the time I lie in the plastic bed and watch my left hand opening and closing without feeling.

**WHILST I** am lying in the hospital bed, the walls I have known in this world begin to crumble. I receive a series of calls from friends with words that swirl – cancer, surgery, chemotherapy, car accident. People I know are dying.

Instead of Christmas and New Year's Eve invitations, I receive dates to attend funerals.

I stand in black at the back of large halls and try not to sob. I grab hands with others – white knuckled – and we hug. I press myself into them, just as they do to me, trying to find something to anchor ourselves to. But all of us are haunting these halls like ghosts – the living and the dead.

When people ask how I am, I want to say, *I'm not doing very well*. I feel eerie and strange, like the sky before a storm, but I know no more than that, and hear the words escape my mouth – *I'm fine*.

I don't tell anyone I still can't feel my left hand. I can't hold a pen. My phone. A bag. That I was released from the hospital with appointments for neurologists and more CT scans, and the word idiopathic scrawled across every page. *Without known cause*.

People I don't know are dying too. It is splashed daily across the news. Murdered for being gay. For being the wrong religion. For being in the wrong place at the wrong time. I find it hard to sleep at night and lie awake blinking at the ceiling, replaying images of global terror attacks, plane crashes and beheadings.

We are at the hands of fate. A few nodules in your arm that grow differently and find places to cluster – liver, brain, bone. Everywhere the world reminds us; we are not in control. I try not to, but at night, I think about my friends, their cold bodies pressed deep into the earth. Decaying. And the others shoved into a cement box at the crematorium. Burning.

I want to pry open the life I had – that girl I was in Europe: full of life's sap, the gloriousness of happiness – just as you crack open a chestnut after it is roasted by the fire. Warm and wondrous, the cracking takes a slight twist of hand – for something that wants to open will spring ajar with the slightest of touch.

But nothing opens. The chestnuts are small and hard. Impenetrable.

I try to think of trees – old pines, London planes (my favourite). The trees that held me as a child. I close my eyes – *remember, remember*. But instead of being under their branches – the leaves moving about in the wind as if shaking out a secret – it is as if I am watching them from inside, a thick pane of glass dividing us, the window firmly locked. It won't budge, and they're just a picture, a painting – no sound, no sound. I can't remember how they smelled in summer, or spring when they budded. I can't remember how the trunk of them felt against my back. I can't remember anything.

*I can't feel anything anymore.*

**THE WORLD** itself goes mad too. It storms and gusts. Gushes of wind and rain pound my window. Outside the palms bend sideways; their fronds flail in the wind. Storm water drains churn and froth, regurgitating mouthfuls of bark and old leaves and sodden plastic bags.

Flowerpots overturn, garden chairs blow into each other, a large Japanese maple lies sideways in someone's garden, roots dangling in the air like legs trying to find ground. I watch as the trees are ripped of leaves, their brittle branches like skeleton fingers pointing upwards into the sky, directing the wind.

People shut themselves inside. Lock doors. Fasten windows. They stay off the roads. They message and mumble, 'I don't remember it ever storming like this in March.'

But to me it is the only thing that makes sense. I open every window in my place. The winds bring in the rain and make everything smell refreshingly of dirt and earth and leaf muck.

But it isn't enough. I need to be out there. *I need to stand in it.*

The white tiled patio is ankle deep in water. My right foot first. Dipping tentatively, like I am getting into an incredibly hot bath. Then my left. Cold lapping at me.

I wade out. Deeper. Until the eaves of the roof no longer protect me and I am in the storm's full force. Thunder rolls and breaks above my head. Winds scurry and whip my hair. The rain plasters my clothes, sodden in seconds. I can't hear. I can't see. I stand there for minutes. Maybe longer. Sopping and saturated. Teeth chattering.

But when I step back inside, dripping, something has washed away.

The storms are followed by incredibly still days – blue skies not broken by a wisp of cloud, no breeze. Temperatures drop, and the birds roost somewhere unheard. The muck and debris begins to dry on the road, but because of the road slicks, people stay inside, warming themselves around heaters, hibernating. It is a strange lull, as though we have been put on hold. Time appears to stop.

I need something else. To go somewhere else. To not be *here*. But where?

Without thinking, I begin to collect maps. Latvia. Finland. Uruguay. India. China. Antarctica. Alaska.

I unfold travel magazines and look at pictures of floating flower markets on barges and misty river mornings. Kayaking with orcas. Giant squid searches in New Zealand. Deep-sea fishing off America. Trekking the Camino. Floating across the Dead Sea.

I ascend into local libraries, finding the complete volumes of everyone that had ever travelled, and sought re-creation. Frances Mayes who gave up her house in America and moved, on a whim, to an old Tuscan villa, beginning a beautiful love affair with Italy; all of her pages smell like flour and semolina and summer leaves of basil. Thoreau who decided he had had enough of civil life and its strange suburban ideals (and this was in 1800s), walked into the woods, where he lived in a small, leaky hut for two years, two months and two days. He scrutinised things no other person had time to pay attention to: the bobbing action of a bluebird, pinecones, shades of a night sky, oak trees, the smell of winter coming. He suggested that everyone should walk in the wild for at least four hours a day – or risk a certain madness.

On my walks around the street at night, lit by lamps instead of moon, swallowed by the roar of car engines half-conversations trail out of people's kitchen windows:

'Did you get the butter?'

'He wants to audit the lot.'

'Harry! Put down your sister's head!'

I am walking, but it is hardly Thoreau's wild. He would have turned up at my doorstep, cussed a little, grabbed my hand and led me deep into his woods – so thick and dense I'd barely be able to see my hand in front of my face.

I paper my fridge and freezer in the red dunes of Namibia and the mountains of Uganda, where there are miles and miles of nature and jungle and dust. Where man has not fenced. Or governed. Or plotted. I long to stand in a place with no walls, no fences. A place that is wild.

Each night, I stare at those postcards papered across my freezer door. Botswana. Zambia. Namibia. Thoreau sits atop my kitchen counter, with a straw hat, strokes his beard with large earth hands, smells of leaf litter and sweat, and whispers, *Grow wild according to thy nature.*

I wander in and out of my house, stand on my balcony, see the street light opposite shine into my bedroom window. Thoreau is busy naming plants in my kitchen.

When I come back inside I already know: I need a way to slip underneath the world as I know it, and reset my life from the inside out.

**WINTER IS** bitterly cold when I purchase a bottle-green backpack, a few pairs of lightweight cargo pants that zip off at the knee and a new pair of hiking boots. My mother urges me to take an old fisherman's hat, for the sun. I squash it under layers of rolled-up singlet tops and windproof, rain-resistant Gore-Tex jackets.

I book my flight on the first day of August. It happens to coincide with *Imbolc* on the pagan calendar, which marks the midway point between winter solstice and spring equinox. A day that celebrates the wild goddess, the earth. A day that offers the power of renewal, rebirth, regeneration.

Although not superstitious, I enjoy the rhythm of cycles and traditions, the soothing effect of ritual. So after the sun sets and the briny cold of winter's night takes up space, sitting in the corner of my house with bone-chilling breath, the outside wind making the foundations and frame squeak like old skeletons raising, I go around the house, lighting candles and turning on lamps, the gas heaters too, filling the house with the promise of light.

I am now the planner of plans, the mapper of maps, the dreamer, the plotter, the doer. How different it feels to be this person again. That spring reappears in my step, and I hum and sing while making dinner.

I take the time to create a hearty sauce from scratch. Tomatoes from the plant on the patio, small and tough-skinned but ready to burst with ripe garlic crushed under the knife. Flakes of salt, onions diced to fine translucent scales, handfuls of basil, their leafy stems lifting the scent of Tuscany to my nose.

I open a green book. I fill the inside with booklets and itineraries, my leaving date, my flight time, a note to myself to buy sunscreen, and still there are pages white and unmarked. I trace the map and the route I would take.

Starting in Kenya, the overland tour truck would traverse the northern tip of Uganda. A week later, we'd dip our toes into Rwanda, with only a little time to scurry back almost the same way before plunging south to Tanzania. A detour north-east off the cape of Dar es Salaam to the spice island of Zanzibar before continuing south, where we'd drop below the equator through Malawi, Zambia and Zimbabwe.

Heading due west, we'd enter Botswana and pause for a few days in her delta before navigating Namibia's barren Skeleton Coast, a resting place of ships and seal bones. From there, we would make our final descent into South Africa, finishing on the south coast where the two mighty oceans, the South Atlantic and Indian, run into each other at Cape Agulhas.

I look at the map for hours, tracing the lines of rivers, the fall of valleys, the places where my feet would stand on the edge of cliffs.

My backpack is stuffed with clothes and lies at the end of my bed, a rolled mat and the smallest sleeping bag I can find strapped loftily to the bottom. I have to be careful slinging the twelve kilograms onto my back – if I begin off balance, the slightest waver could make me lose my step.

The night before I leave, I am too alert to sleep. But too tired to read. I try a few sentences of Keats and the words blur and become a map of Africa, black and waiting. I kick off the blankets and curl up in a small side chair, under the window. I decide to wait all night for the sun to rise. I open the window and the winter air tumbles in like a wave, breaking against my walls. I blink; I breathe. The sky itself, is a stretch of black, I can't tell shape or form, it could begin just at the tip of my nose – or somewhere far away, far above.

Silence falls like a shroud. I wonder if I've suddenly become deaf. I tap my finger on my window sill to know – tap, tap, tap – I can still hear. Everything else is rinsed away, swallowed in sky; it is an abyss. Then a creeping shadow. A huge dome. A crushed velvet throw rug. My back starts to ache. My toes are numb and icy. I'm about to give up, try and get some sleep, when she emerges: the sun. Spine first, arched and heaving, pulling herself over the ridge of night. Light spreads in strands at first. Then lashes my walls with buttery gold.

I take a hot shower. Somewhere a kookaburra laughs. I pull on my new Gore-Tex shirt and it feels like someone has knitted together air – it's as light against my skin as if I were wearing a gown of dandelions. Someone next door asks for more milk in their coffee. The night is small and cold behind me, almost forgotten. When the clock chimes six, I pick up my backpack, and slide back into the world.

# AFRICA

**NAIROBI'S STICKY** season. The summer sun blankets the earth like hot honey. Within seconds, sweat pools under my arms and in the cups of my bra. It runs down my back and I swat at it like a pesky fly.

Everything sticks to me: a local lady's sweat as she leans across to grab her bag from the squeaking conveyer belt; leaking water from the rusted air conditioning; a man's raspy uncovered cough. In five minutes, I am covered by the viscous sap of this land.

Outside the airport, it's a riot of noise. Constant plane traffic. Jet engines. Car horns peel like vuvuzelas at a rowdy soccer match. The beep of motorbikes roaring past. Somewhere near the airport a building site, the clang of metal upon metal, men shouting and then the gnarling pound of a drill that seems to tear through road and rock. The whole place appears to shake. My entire body weak and weary, my mind floating and slow after being above the cloud line for thirty hours.

A line of old white taxis sit in the heat; paint peeling, bald tyres and rusted roofs. Drivers stand in a group under the only, gnarled tree, cigarettes in one hand, flicking away flies with the other. The wind lifts their smell towards me; sour sweat and cheap tobacco.

One of them approaches with a smile, flicks his butt into the sand and holds out his hand. Tyam. His palm is warm and dry, and mine sweats into his.

'Sorry,' I say, wiping my hands on my t-shirt.

He heaves my pack into his rusted boot. The seats in the back are missing springs and sag in the middle like old skin. The passenger seat has a rip through the leather as if someone with a knife has slit from the headrest to the floor. I straddle it awkwardly.

The air conditioning is broken. I wind the window down as far as it will go. As we leave the airport, something in the distance is burning and the smell of scorched rubber fills my lungs.

We turn sharply onto a four-lane highway. Cars surge past us. Mercedes and BMWs with rusted paint, dirty exhaust coughs and no side mirrors. The drivers enthusiastically press their horns, leaning on them longer than necessary. The streets become a dissonant rumble.

Along the highway small stores open their doors. People shop for fresh tomatoes, piles of melons, ripening bananas. Small cafes look busy. People sit in plastic white chairs at small, card-sized tables surrounded by crates of Coke and Fanta stacked high against faded blue walls. There's a hardware store. A truck mechanic. Off to the left a large white building sprawls across several blocks. Tyam points to it, a shopping mall. Air conditioned. I think how delicious it would be to stand in a blast of cool air, if only for a few seconds.

Tyam changes lanes with a jerk, stopping suddenly for a car without working tail lights, flinging us both forward. The brakes scream; there's the grinding of metal. My stomach makes a sound like it's being strangled. I gulp a mouthful of warm water from my backpack, and stick my face closer to the open window.

As soon as I'd landed on Kenya's tarmac I expected to feel a sense of promise and relief because I was moving again. Going somewhere. As if travelling itself is a tonic, a tincture, that can be poured into you the moment you step off a plane.

But it isn't.

I feel strange, overtired. I'm about to be sick. It could be jet lag. Or the smell of rubbish burning. *Blllopp*. My stomach churns. *Must get out*, I think.

I ask Tyam to stop for a minute, so I can walk a bit. He says no, it's not safe, and locks the doors with a central switch.

Ten minutes later we hit solid traffic. Bumper to bumper. The taxi wheezes and shudders as we shift into lowest gear.

It becomes unbearably hot when we aren't moving. My thighs stick together and to the leather seat. My sweaty hands continually slip off my legs and fall against the burning leather. The stick shift starts to melt under the sun's full force.

Up ahead, local men stand on the side of the road with armfuls of pink plastic sunglasses, paper fans, fake flowers, to sell to passing cars, like a moving bric-a-brac market. One man is holding out a black puppy to the traffic. He looks like Mufasa on Pride Rock lifting up Simba. *Is he selling it?*

Most of them have ripped pants, old and stained. No shoes. *Do they make enough to eat*, I wonder. *To have homes?*

We inch forward, then stop. The men spot me through the open window. A tourist. They make a beeline for our car. A man with plastic flowers arrives first. He sticks the fake flowers through my open window as though they're real and he wants me to smell their aroma.

'No thanks.'

'A pair of plastic lime-green sunglasses?'

'No thanks.'

'A tray for ice cubes?'

I look away. I wasn't sure what else to do to stop them coming.

Tyam stares idly out his window, as though this window shopping is quite usual.

More hands shove through the window. Scarves. Postcards. Carved statues of elephants small enough to fit in my pocket.

But I don't need more things to put in my pocket. They have been full for so long, with receipts and bills and business cards and appointment slips and lip gloss and hair clips and all the things I convinced myself were essential, but as it turns out, I didn't need at all.

Space. That's what I need.

A man with a terracotta pot, chipped and spilling dirt in a trail behind him, approaches slowly. He has a limp and appears to be dragging part of his foot across the hot tar.

He pushes the pot through the window, presenting it as if the closer it is, the more chance I'll buy it.

The pot is red and broken. Inside, an old dry fern is giving up on life. She has grown a good few inches, perhaps gold and green once, before the sun raged against her. As if in hope, she had birthed two more fronds and then decided against it, and they had curled over, shedding themselves. Their burnt stems now lay shrivelled and hard, still attached, but past resurrection.

*I'll take it!* I think. I know I can give life back to this fern, simply by adding a bit of water. Talking to it. Putting it in the shade for a while. Wouldn't it then spring back to life?

But what use do I have for a pot out here? We've been told by the tour guides to pack little, and even then, halve it. The pot would take up half my backpack, and then what use are we to each other?

I sit for a few seconds in silence. Why am I so fixated on buying this plant? Surely I'm better off with the plastic sunglasses. Or the battery-operated face fan in the shape of strawberry.

I'm just about to open my mouth and say *no thanks* when I look at the seller. He's a hunched, old, wizened man. His mouth like a shrivelled plum sucked into space, a black hole behind where his teeth should be. His wrinkled hands shake as though he has advanced Parkinson's, causing the dirt to spill across the road and my lap.

I rummage around in my bag and pull out ten dollars from my wallet, handing it to him. He pushes the pot into my hands.

*No, no,* I shake my head.

'Thank you, thank you.' He smiles toothlessly at me, nods and says, 'Where you going?'

I pause. I could say the name of the hotel but I don't want him to know I am headed to a place with pools and lush gardens. I feel guilty I am going there at all. I could say Uganda. Or Rwanda. Or Nairobi's centre.

But he has kind, deep brown eyes that somehow look inside me, and I wonder if he knows I don't know where I am going.

'I don't know,' I say quietly, thinking, *how true*.

The traffic ahead starts to move. He steps back. We move forward at a snail's crawl, braking regularly, before eventually speeding up.

When I look back, I'm not sure why. To wave to the plum-mouthed man? To see him again? Perhaps to make sure he has found safety as the cars start to speed past. But, of course, he has. He has lived here for years, this place has made him. Shaped him.

Arriving at the Hotel Sarova Pacifica, Tyam takes in my bags and I tip him generously. I tell the front desk clerk I'm here for the overland trip. She smiles and says to meet downstairs just after dawn.

I fall gratefully into room 212's tight, white bed sheets. My head pounds. The air conditioning is switched on high and the buzz fills the room like a swarm of flies. Outside the pool lights burst into the night, casting shadows from the palm trees that lumber into the sky.

When I close my eyes I think about the plum-mouthed man and his fern. I think about the sound his bad foot had made, a coarse shuffle, as it was pulled across the road. And in that small space between consciousness and sleep, I'm thankful that everything is moving again, lest we become potted and flailing and giving up on life.

**WHEN I** arrive downstairs at dawn, the hotel driveway is crammed with white people and backpacks. It looks like summer camp. I think, *Oh God, I can't do this.*

I escape inside and drink a watermelon juice from the breakfast bar. Outside, people shake hands and exchange names. They laugh and chat and greet each other like old friends. A stocky girl with a large smile, long black hair and beautiful island skin, a milky caramel, is telling people where to go, where to put packs, and sleeping bags and tents and bread.

I order another watermelon juice and then need the toilet.

When it's almost time for the bus to leave, I decide I will go. I have to sprint before they close the door. My backpack, the last one, is stowed in the bulk hold.

Inside Matilda, our cobalt blue truck, there is the smell of lemon antiseptic, bleach, damp carpet and anticipation. People say names and smile. *Hello, hello.* Another Aussie, they say and shake their heads, as if we are multiplying like rabbits. I slip into the first empty seat.

The girl next to me says, 'I'm Antonia,' in a posh, clipped English accent, 'but call me Ant.' With young skin and perfect, wavy, blonde hair tumbling half way down her back, she has the finely boned face of a bird

– beautiful and elegant. She would be better placed in a full-page Hilfiger ad than in a tent.

Eager friends sitting across from us introduce themselves as Pip and Shamil from Melbourne. This trip marks their last holiday before they graduate as doctors. Ant says she has just graduated as an environmental scientist from Auckland University, and has spent the last several months exploring the Middle East.

'What about you?' they ask, and expectant eyes fall on me.

They want to know what I do for work. Saying *change manager* makes my mouth feel as if it was stuffed with cotton wool. It makes people think of sweeping boardrooms and marble floors, high heels and matching suit jackets, and meetings about strategies and operational models. And that is a person even I don't know.

Here's a word I want to say. *Writer*. But that word elicits the same questions. Every time.

'Books?' they say.

'Yes.'

'What kind? Fiction?'

'No, actually, non-fiction.'

'Oh, what about?'

'Life.'

They laugh a bit here before they realise I'm serious.

'So have you had anything published?'

'Not yet.'

'Oh.'

Always that response. *Oh.* There is the weight of the world in disappointment in that *Oh*.

I suppose I could tell them about the novella I'd written, the book of poetry too, but I self-published them, and people look a bit twitchy when I mention self-publishing. Isn't that what writers who can't get a publishing deal do?

They're looking at me, so I say quickly, 'I'm just here to see some lions.'

They laugh. As they do, Ant sits back and I catch sight of my reflection in the truck windows. A slumped face that hasn't slept a full night in years.

I suddenly feel old. Sagging and tired. What am I doing on a tour with all these young people? I can taste the acid again in my throat. I start to fret. *I'm not sure I can do this*, I think, watching our guide Sarah slam the rusty truck doors and slide the safety chain from the outside, locking us together.

Matilda's engine turns on, roaring so loudly we can't talk anymore. I feel relieved. The truck moves heavily and slowly down the driveway like an elephant risen from slumber. Slowly we lurch forward to join the Nairobi traffic. High in the trees vultures circle and nest. Wrinkled pink skin heads. Sharp eyes, seeing things we can't.

Rubbish spills across the road. There are bottles and packets and plastic bags aplenty. The vultures have put much of this to good use – blue bottle tops, lolly wrappers and silver foil glint from the nests overhead. What remains of old rubbish – leftover meat and rotten vegetables – begins to heat under the sun. The flies buzz as they happily find new places to lay their maggot eggs.

For hours, when we move it can be measured in inches. Roll. Stop. Roll. Stop. It's hot inside the truck. Someone suggests we open the top windows. The warm breeze streams in, bringing gifts of sand. In minutes, everything is coated as though we've been sitting in a closed room for decades and need a good dusting. When the winds pick up, the sand hits our faces like a million pins, stinging our cheeks, so we close them again.

On the edge of the city we peel off and leave the gridlock. Matilda wheezes to a gallant eighty kilometres an hour, which in a truck that size feels as if we are about to take off.

Outside the city, everything is stained brown. Russet roadside cliffs. Broad boulders. Dark umber dirt. Scrawny trees, bark shredded from their limbs waving in the breeze. Dead branches fallen on each other, rolling about like lusty lovers in the dusty flats. The day is brilliant; blue skies and the fierceness of the sun. Warm and comfortable, I nod gently into a dozing sleep.

'Zebra!' someone shouts. I'm suddenly awake. All conversation stops. People jostle to find bags, switch cameras on and shove them out the smudged windows. Flocks of zebras stand along the highway swatting flies with their tails. People lift their cameras at every opportunity, trying to capture monochromatic rumps with zoomed lenses.

Someone jerks open the sliding window to get a better view. The breath of Kenya roars in; tossing our hair, stinging our eyes and silently slipping between our lips.

**THE GREAT** Rift Valley is located between the mountains, Kenya and Kilimanjaro, and knows the damage a fierce love affair can do. It is the longest rift on earth, and the eldest. Formed between two and seven million years ago, it stretches along the earth's crust from Syria to Mozambique, running through Ethiopia, Tanzania, Congo, Malawi, Jordan and the Middle East, some 6000 kilometres in length.

Wind and water are not the only elements culpable in creating this massive rift, for the playing of middle earth is also to blame.

Millions of years ago, two tectonic plates could not decide, quite like lovers, whether they wished to be passionate or parted. They came together. They separated. They reconciled again. And while they bickered underneath ancient hominid feet, this toing and froing created bulges above.

Fight after fight, they caused the earth's crust to weaken, to swell, and to build. Until one day they erupted – a lovers' fight – and the earth's crust could not hold on any longer. One side dropped, faulted. It gave way, tearing a line for a million miles, ripping across the earth's crust like a giant's zipper split open.

When the rift arrived in Kenya it couldn't decide which way to go, and quite like the dual minds of lovers it diverged, offering us the possibility of going west or east. To choose our own path.

The western rift curves along the backbone of Kenya. Scooping lower than the valleys, over time it filled with water, and became known as the African Great Lakes. To the east, the rift is shorter and, as viewed on a map, is the shape of a wishing bone before it is ceremoniously torn.

If you choose to take the eastern, wishbone route, along the escarpments that rise 2500 metres over the valley, you may find yourself standing on the edge of the rift. Much like the edge where I find myself standing now.

An imposing sky, blue and forever, stretches like a bolt of silk unfurled above. A sheer drop, precarious and rocky, falls to a floor of desert, laid flat like an old dusty carpet. In parts the earth splits, and bare rock juts from the ground like broken bones poking through skin.

Across the desert floor, wind-whipped eddies spin. Devil dust storms. They gather and circle like mini tornadoes, furiously whirling, before collapsing exhausted, falling to the ground, dropping their carriage of sand and stone.

The wind howls up the rocky cliffs bringing gusts of sand and dirt that pelt our face. The gusts rework the side of the cliffs like an artist who is never happy, stopping to view its work, a sliver of silence, before it starts again, furiously carving.

Masai blankets in scarlet red and lined with bold blue hang over wire, flapping in the breeze. Each end hurtles towards the other, letting out an almighty snap, cracking like a whip. A Kenyan man sits on the ground, whittling away, chip chip, creating a rhino from a solid block of wood.

'You want elephant?' The toothless man with big eyes laughs. *Come. Look. Buy.*

'Maybe later,' I say, and walk in the opposite direction.

The fence, rickety and rotted, separates us from the sheer drop below. *Don't lean.* Sheer heat rises from the trough below, steaming up like we've lifted the top off a boiling pan of water and put our face in it.

Down below more dusty devil whirlwinds rise like zombies from the grave, and begin to thrash across the plains. I look eastward over the scorched brown land where nothing grows. Beneath my feet, layers of lives lie upon each other, one after the other. All those stories. All those people. So much force and life under my feet. Under this earth. Right here.

I sit on the edge and dangle my feet over and gravity a hundred miles down, tugs at me. My shoes feel like they have little weights in them.

Who else has stood here? Battled here? Bled here? Died here? Can I feel it – if I close my eyes and try hard – can I feel the sense of others folded together in the soil, all of us coming together?

Here is something I could spend a lifetime considering: the theory of eternalism – that the past, present and future is not real; instead, everything is happening, all at once. Time, some scientists say, doesn't exist at all. This constructer, that we have carefully plotted our entire lives around, isn't even real. And if this is to be believed, right now on this place I'm sitting, Lucy, the first primate human, is being dug up and discovered, the rift is emerging, herds of bison are migrating, ancient Mombasan tribes are discovering the land, sowing it with seeds and fruit, and somewhere across the seas Pompeii is going down in flames and lava.

Rumour is this theory will be proven right. That our earth is indeed is one giant time-space dimension. I try to get my head around it – this theory that everything is happening right now.

If this is true, I may stay awhile here, see if I can't gaze into the distance, let reality become a little hazy. See instead what I can make out. Reach around the edges of things we thought were long out of grasp, and hold them again.

Perhaps we don't need to worry about the ever-constant beat of time, measuring out the portions of our life. Thoreau said he lived like the Puri Indians, who have one word for today, yesterday and tomorrow. Who do not fret about the ticking of the clock, or the incessant need to fill time. Instead, Thoreau measured moments: wild flowers opening, fluttering of poplar leaves, the grace of mornings, crows flying two or three abreast, heavy thunder-showers that kept him inside – and all of it gave him the feeling of delight.

The wind picks up. Warm like breath. The summer sun, large and grand, pulls closer to the earth, marking mid-day. The man with no teeth starts whistling softly. Ant finds me and sits down silently, letting her legs dangle over the side too.

I wonder, what does she see?

The dust winds. The Arabs arriving. The British colonies during the First World War. I tilt my head to the sky and watch a cluster of crows flocking in a V-shape across the sky.

Maybe anything is not only possible but probable. But more than that – it is happening and happened and is about to happen.

**THERE ARE** certain roads we can follow through Lake Nakuru. Across the park towards the water buffalo. Under the cloistered trees in the hope of seeing solitary leopards.

It's a bright afternoon. The grass hasn't seen rain in years. Bleached yellow tufts, sharp and crunchy like spinifex, have baked too long in earth's oven. Sweat lingers on everyone's brow and arms are pushed out of windows hoping for a breeze. On the ground, old leaves are paper thin and sun-curled. Perfect conditions for a bushfire.

Our tyres create large clouds of smoke and dust. Each time we stop it takes minutes to settle, for us to be able to see again, as dust and stone settle into new places. When it does, someone points out the way light is hitting the rocks.

Then a small fleck of ebony down by the lake – could it be a rare black rhino? There are *oohs* and *ahhs* and camera clicks just like we are viewing a painting in an art gallery. Matilda rumbles closer. Apparently we've scared him, because just as we get close enough, he turns and runs in the opposite direction. Quite daintily too, for something that weighs over 800 kilograms.

We drive further around Lake Nakuru towards the flat fields. These fields could be anywhere in the world, except they also couldn't because meerkats quickly run past Matilda. We're going at a snail's pace, but even so the driver slams on the brakes like we're a rally car hitting a hidden hairpin curve. The meerkats stand to attention as though we're about to be introduced. As if there are hands to shake.

For a second they look at us. Frozen. Then, as if forgotten, they run a metre away. Tumble over each other. One stands post like a sentinel – stony and silent. One starts playing with another's tail like it's a hot piece of toast, tossing it between each hand before dropping it triumphantly on the ground. A game of tails. They switch roles. More join, wanting to get in on the hot toast tail game. Suddenly they all freeze. Stand up straight. Ears cocked. *What is it?* Noses twitch, eyes wide. *What is it?* A few seconds of pause. Nothing happens. Danger forgotten, they return to scampering, jostling in lines. Polishing each other's fur. When we leave, they don't even notice.

At the lake's edge pink flamingos perch silently. Hundreds of them, legs folded or lifted like graceful ballerinas in a delicate pose. Elegantly, one by one, they unfold their bodies, tilting their heads to the ground, sipping water. A group of them take flight, propelling legs so quickly on the lake's surface they find traction where other animals would fall and splash. Stretching their necks, they lean forward, their wings catch the wind and they lift, with ease, into the air. In flight they glide silently, large pointed wing spans, dove-white on top, galah pink on the bottom.

We round the lake and head off into thick woodland where the shadows are cooling. Someone with amazing vision asks the truck to stop (bang the cabin twice) because they've spotted an owl. An owl who should probably be asleep given it's still early afternoon, but instead is sitting silently on a branch, hooded eyes watching us. It's hard to see him at first, his soft grey and brown feathers camouflaging him among the tree canopy.

*What is life like for something designed to be hidden?*

I focus my camera and try to capture him. Instead I take sharp photos of leaves and a greyish owl blob in the background. I try again and this time capture the rounded hood of his eyes, the black beads staring off into the distance, the rim of white feathers on his face. I wonder if I was to return to this world, if I may enjoy being a hooded eyed owl with a perfect view of Lake Nakuru.

Back into a clearing, a field seems to stretch forever. Only at the last moment, our eyes see the horizon rising sharply into a large peak. Is it a mountain? In Australia, we'd call it a mountain. If we were in Canada or France, they'd take one look at this and likely say it's a small hill. Emphasis on the small.

White rhinos are everywhere. Dozens of them sitting, lying, eating, breathing, standing. Birds perched on their backs. It feels like I'm watching an episode of *Planet Earth* but here, in real life, it's brilliant. All this, this wildness, is mesmerising. I don't want to move on, but we do.

Off in the distance the creamy, old English toffee rumps of giraffes dot the horizon. Closer, a herd of playful gazelles. They stand together almost in line, rump side facing us, two white half-circles on either rear quarter, joined by a long white tail that flits puppy-like, side to side.

The gazelles raise their heads suddenly. Jerk. Noses twitch. Tails stand stiff and still. There is danger lurking in the grass. We stare into the dense undergrowth. Our eyes make branches into snakes, and mounds of dirt into lurking hyenas. Sun and shade are tricksters; they make things of nothing and just as easily are able to conceal almost everything.

The gazelles retreat quickly, prancing to the left disappearing into undergrowth. *Is that a lion?* We strain our necks. Without the animal instinct so necessary out here to see what can't be seen, all I can see are the powerful rays of sunlight breaking through clouds, leaving the rest of the hill shrouded in the shadows of late afternoon.

**OUR ITINERARY** suggests we camp in Nakuru Park, giving us the thrill of hearing the night sounds of Africa's famous wild beasts.

When I read this, I imagined a central campsite covered by a canopy of woven African trees, perhaps a fence or three, some barbed wire (only as a barrier) and a raised platform to view the animals as they kept to their area and we kept to ours. What I didn't imagine was setting up tents in the middle of the park – there are no divides, no us and them areas, and no fences.

Our campsite is a small clearing. Trees shroud one side. Pit toilets at one end, the haze of the lake in the distance, a clove of trees bushy and briared to the far east, places that Sarah our guide tells us we don't want to walk into either with intent or by accident.

In there, the canopy is so dense that even in the height of day not one ray of sunlight can push through. And at night, well, there are the formidable under-the-bed nightmares awaiting us. Except these things would be very real. A snake in your hair. A dangling hairy spider. A lion or two hungry and roaming. No, these are not places we should go, she warns.

*Unmapped and unmarked.*

I stare at the thick forest and think it looks rather wonderful.

We're quickly put to work before we lose the sunlight. Some are tasked with gathering wood and layering it to make a fire across an old shallow pit. I'm on kitchen duty. We peel avocados, slice each of them open, and carve their slippery flesh. We add lemon zest and limes (the last we will see for a while), chopped tomatoes bought this morning from the local markets, and liberal dashes of cumin, both ground and smoked.

Sarah takes to the makeshift kitchen, creating amazing meals out of nothing. She sizzles minced beef with onion and garlic, packets of corn chips toasted slightly on pans above the fire. A can of kidney beans with oil and garlic for the vegetarians. We create a bowl of guacamole for twenty people so big my face could fit in it. The fire roars and the chips are done within seconds. We remove them quickly before they blacken and char.

We eat quickly by the fire, hunched over and spooning mouthfuls of chili con carne, before it gets cold on our plastic plates. Before the sun slips away and I watch the green buds on trees become black. There is a last ribbon of milky white that hovers for a while, a band between the earth and the heavens, as the sun finally loses her hold on the sky. She slides quickly, and we are covered in night.

Once the sky turns a deep indigo and the night is lit by a smattering of stars, it becomes chilly. The glaring hot surface of the world is long forgotten. The animals change and those on night shift – the mosquitos and insects – begin to buzz in our ears, and land on uncovered flesh. Our hands, our fingers, the creamy skin exposed between sweater and pants.

By the fire everyone looks the same, silhouettes huddled in hoodies and beanies, the occasional flicker of firelight on faces. After the brilliance of sunshine, my body quickly feels the deepening cold, low in my stomach. I keep yawning into my palm. When there's a lull, I slip quietly away from the fire and the stories shared over the lick of flames.

How dark it is out here. I dare not navigate my way to the pit toilets in this nocturnal shade. Even with the help of a head torch, I decide to hold on. Inside the small two-man tent I share with Ant, I undress quickly and slide between the ruffled layers of my sleeping bag. It smells of newness and cold. I choose to lay my head not on a pillow or clothes, but straight on the tent floor. Here, I breathe in dirt and soil and the places lions have trod, and my heart

Only a thin veil separates me from the earth – the place I have come to explore.

**HRPHH. HRPHH.** Hrphh. The shuffling of giants outside. Hrphh. Giants moving things, like they're reshaping the world.

When I poke my head through a small portion of unzipped tent, the noise stops. Then starts again. Hrphh. Hrphh.

The world has a slight chill. The breeze brings a honey hay flavour, most likely from the loose tussock grasses. I can still smell smoke from the glowing coals of last night's fire. No-one else stirs. Matilda's silhouette looks like an overgrown blue giant, squatting in the yard. I can just make out the peaks of the other tents, clustered in a tight circle.

It takes my eyes a full minute to adjust to the darkness on this moonless night. The stars are the only things lighting the ground, and they do so timidly.

When my eyes begin to make shapes out of the darkness, I notice several hirsute baboons waiting on the camp's edge. They hold our tents under watchful gaze. One perches on a log in a Buddha squat. Another in table top yoga pose, with rounded fists pounded deep into the earth, the third playing with his foot, his back facing us. The two alert baboons change places, hands fisted and thumping into the earth like they're playing the whack-a-mole game at a state fair. Hrphh. Hrphh. I lie watching them for a few minutes, my eyes adjusting to the pre-dawn darkness.

I can't stop looking at the baboons. I wonder too, if they've spotted me. The lady with her head horizontally pushed through a tent. But I can't stay too long like this, or I'll be walking around with a strange sore neck all day.

We've been pre-warned about baboons. They are partial to anything with a fragrance. Perfumes. Lip gloss. Toothpaste. As long as everything has a lid screwed on tight, there's no need for concern. But accidentally leave the lid just a little askew, and these baboons with amazing noses can sniff it a mile away. *Could they smell the toothpaste I used last night? The paw paw ointment I smeared on my lips?*

There are stories of baboons who chased people from the bathroom, or tried to join them in the shower. Or unzipped their tents while the owners were at breakfast and on returning found the baboons inside their tent – clothes strewn everywhere, toothpaste lids removed. Tubes squashed and pressed and licked like dessert. Apparently one even had a pair of pink underwear laying across his head like a slanted hat.

The baboons sit still for a moment, as though paused. They sit lumpish and rather like humans. Had I not stared at them well, but rather glimpsed at them, I could have thought them rather hairy campers, taking the time to stare about under the stars. Night walkers like me who can't sleep until the dawn, even if they wanted to.

Finally they wander off towards the trees and deep undergrowth. First dawn breaks through. Tiny clumps of clouds gather. The early sun tinting them sugar pink, like marshmallows. It's still early. My watch says 5 am. I close my eyes and wish for more sleep.

Mostly, I want to stand under a shower of strong, hot water. But there is no shower, no trickle of water, no bathrooms. The only way I can get clean is a once-moist baby wipe that's now old and dry and feels like scrunched paper on my skin.

Changing is another hurdle. I try to put on a singlet top while standing under a plastic roof the height of my bottom rib. I am stooped from the middle like a grandma with osteoporosis. Somehow I manage to find a way to lie on my back and pull on cargo pants, my feet floating in the air like a dead bug. All of this must be completed without a trace of noise, for Ant is deep in slumber just several inches away.

In the grey ashy morning, early risers are huddled round the fire, spearing pieces of bread and holding it over the ashes, making smoked toast. I make a mug of bitter coffee without milk, and throw in several teaspoons of clumpy sugar.

As the sun rises, the colour of the sky changes rapidly. Peach fuzz, a blast of orange. Then bright, lemony and hot, flattening the clouds. By eight, it's pure daylight, brazen and glaring.

We drive slowly out of the park, leaving dust in our wake. Matilda sways and finds her balance on the uneven track. Beads of sweat glow on each of us.

When I look back, dots of lake water spray everywhere. Tens of thousands of flamingos foraging in the shallow blue waters of the lake, ascend, wings stretched. The sky is a rush of pink. If you look closely, a fish escapes his watery house for a second – discovers the roar of sky, the cluster of wings – dives back in.

**OUR FIRST** country town. We stop briefly in the bustling centre. A crowd gathers at the truck door; postcards are waved in our faces like fans. Ebony giraffes float against the truck windows like flying unicorns. There is a circle of men at the door yelling Look! Look! Holding up black caps that say KENYA in embroidered red and green. How do we get out?

Some try and grabble with the crowd, or reason with them. I hear one impossibly polite Belgium lady, asking, 'Could you please let me through, I'd like to use the bathroom.' Ant and I slip through silently, holding each other's hand and ducking down, weaving in a sea of legs, like navigating a dense wood. We skip across the street when there's a break in the traffic.

The metal in old awnings creaks as they heat. Shop doors stay open waiting for gusts of wind to cool them down. Power is unstable, lights flicker and the whir of back-up electricity generators hum loudly. The streets are dusty, the pavements are worn and uneven. People queue in their lunch breaks, spilling outside a peeling white building that says BANK, the line snakes out the door, around the corner and farther down the street beyond. Men in suits joke with one another, women retrieve large wheat-coloured fans from their bag and keep a constant beat aimed at their faces. No-one seems the least put out.

Farther down the street is a church, a block of sparse gravel and grass with some haphazardly placed bricks and old sheet metal, and a hand-painted sign that reads, GYM. We stroll down a long, sloping laneway.

A smiling man in a bright red shirt, has set up a travelling shop; a large blue tarpaulin hammered into the ground is stacked with the most peculiar shoes. An array of sandals and thongs, dark black and spongey. All of them seem so much larger than normal – at least twice the size. Their tips came to a point like elf shoes, rounded into the sky like crescent ebony moons.

'Tyres,' the man says as he introduces himself as Mbita. Holding up a curved shoe proudly he says, 'We collect them by the road.'

We're quite stunned by this invention. There are so many questions. 'How do you make them?'

With knives and a little fire to seal the edges.

'Are there different sizes?'

'Yes. Large and small,' answers Mbita with a wonderful laugh. He seems so interesting, we forget about exploring and want to stay talking instead.

'Do you wear them?'

*Sometimes.*

'Does your family?'

For the first time he doesn't smile. He tells us quietly his wife died recently. He had to pack up his son and two baby girls and move further away, outside the town. Down a long, dusty road. I focus very hard on listening, on looking at the shoes, and try not to think of his children at home in varying stages of motherlessness.

Suddenly Mbita is smiling again. 'Really, they are lovely for your feet,' he says, gesturing to the tyre-shoes.

*Did I want to buy a pair,* he is asking. I can feel the silence between what I want to say – *no thank you* – for what use do I have for tyre-shoes?

And the other answer, the one we are all expecting, 'Yes please, I'll take three pairs.' I keep seeing in my mind the wild eyes of his children wanting something for dinner.

'They're all quite big.' I say slowly. 'And I have enough shoes.'

Mbita nods. 'It's okay,' he says still smiling. 'It's okay.'

I offer instead to pay for a photo of Mbita and his extra-terrestrial sized tyre-shoes. He shrieks with delight, then poses, two thumbs up.

At the bottom of the street, small eateries are busy selling Coke in glass bottles floating in tubs of half-melted ice. Home-cooked ugali, the staple food, a dish of maize flour cooked with water until it forms a porridge or dough-like consistency is the lunchtime special. This is rolled into a lump or ball and is garnished with vegetable stews or, for those with more money, meat stews, where the ugali is dipped into the sauces and acts like a scoop soaking up the flavours around it.

We buy a plate to share and two Cokes. They're warm and the fizz seems to have disappeared a while ago. The cafe owner, a small lady in her fifties, offers a choice of three sides with the ugali – cooked cabbage, wilted spinach, or meat stew. *The first two. Not the meat.*

We sit at a small plastic table near the front of the cafe where we can watch the people come and go along the street. The door is open and the hot breeze slips quickly through, like a current. Flies buzz happily in search of food and use my neck as some sort of airport landing.

The ugali arrives. No forks. No spoons. I don't feel I should be eating with my hands. *God, where had they been? In pit latrines and against walls covered in dust and dirt.* We ask politely for two forks and are given one between us, which we share without thinking – one night in a tent has caused all inhibitions to disappear.

My first bite of ugali is rubbery. Tasteless. I try spooling wilted spinach around it like a ribbon, but then it just tastes wet and rubbery.

'Do you like it?' Ant asks offering me back the fork after nibbling a tiny mouthful.

The lady behind the counter stares and I wonder if she can hear.

I swallow heavily. 'Not for every meal.'

We can't decide whether to keep eating or forget it. Ant takes the fork and dips it into the cooked cabbage, its strands translucent, a strange yellow green. We try not to notice the pigeons who have taken up residence on the table next to us eyeing our plate.

Finally, after passing the fork between us another few times, we leave a tip and take our warm Cokes with us.

**WE DRIVE** for hours along a black tar road pitted with potholes. Everything looks the same. Dirty blonde soil, spindly trees barely thicker than my fingers.

Despite the chill of the early mornings, Kenya heats quickly. Climbing from the truck just before noon, the day smacks my face with heat. The top of Matilda has started to sizzle. Feeling dehydrated, I fill my water bottle from the guts of the truck. The water storage tank can hold litres, and is treated with tablets so the water is drinkable. I take a long sip then immediately spit it onto the dust. It tastes like warm bleach; I'd rather go thirsty.

We set up little fold-out stools in a semicircle, and wooden fold-out tables stored deep within the belly of Matilda are set up for lunch.

Sarah lays out ten loaves of bread, bulk jars of mayonnaise that could fit a human head, a two-litre bottle of tomato sauce, an old jar of mustard and a container of butter – melted and runny like egg yolk. Those on kitchen duty cut up cucumber and carrot with blunt knives, then lay out cold-cuts of meat, pink with large white gristle bits, which is hardly cold at all. Mountains of cheese are grated from solid kilogram blocks. The cheese, a strange bright orange, like layers of waxy carrot.

We line up at the buffet-like trestle tables making sandwiches on brown plastic plates. There are tiny pieces of onion for those who get to it first. No-one is sure if they should touch the cheese. It has already melted into itself forming a bubbling lava trail.

I make a plate of wilted lettuce, cucumber and mustard and pour ketchup over it. When I was younger I'd have sauce on everything. On crackers. On slices of apple. Banana. (Yes, it's true.) And even ice cream. In my mind, there's nothing that can't be made better with tomato sauce. Except, it seems, wilted lettuce.

No-one talks; it's too hot. We push flies away from our face but they keep returning. Some campers go back for seconds but everything is warm, almost hot, and I've seen too many flies resting on the cucumber to do that.

After lunch we pack the tables away, wash the plates that dry in seconds, and take our seats back on the truck.

The earth rolls along. Cities and towns, give way to open land – barren and broken and beautifully spacious. How much would it cost to buy a slice? Could you build a house here? I've always wanted a vegetable garden, a herb potager, but if you try and plant tiny seedlings into this parched ground, the earth could easily push them back up.

When we stop near a vegetable market, I buy a handful of bananas; short and stumpy – each one no longer than my fingers. Just picked, the man tells me. My first mouthful, falls apart like spun sugar in my mouth; tastes of sunshine and sky. It forces my eyes closed. I finish one and eat another.

I think of the bananas I bought in Sydney. Cold like fish, resting on ice. God knows how long they were stored in the supermarket's industrial fridges. I think we all know, but have forgotten, or want to forget that our fresh produce is not so fresh. Apparently, apples store well and can spend up to eighteen months in cool closure, before they're wheeled onto the shop floor, sprayed with water to look fresh, picked and plucked into our trolleys. Broccoli comes out wearing ice chips in their hair. Carrots are chilled. Is it any wonder, tomatoes don't taste like tomatoes anymore? Isn't anyone else worried?

When I leave, I buy another bunch. I think about saving half for dessert, but when Matilda starts moving, I find myself peeling and eating them all, one by one. Down below, a lone zebra trots along the roadside, whisking away invisible flies. The driver of a passing truck, leans out the window, waving at us and tooting his horn. I grin and wave back. After that, we don't see anyone else.

Just ninety hours ago I was buying a tube of travel toothpaste from Priceline in Sydney. I was buying pre-packaged pasta in plastic wrap to cook for dinner. I was cutting a refrigerated apple for breakfast, cool and crunchy, tasting of air, of nothing. I was listening to the marine roar of the traffic hum near my house.

Am I here in Africa? Sometimes, it feels like a dream.

**WE STOP** briefly for the night, at a campsite somewhere in Uganda, arriving after the sun has set.

The intensity of the heat has halved. A chilly wind pushes through. Shadows emerge and the night feels like the breath of winter. The evening grows icy and a rough wind fells our cheeks. Someone makes pasta with steamed carrots. I eat without tasting. Voices and chattering around the fire seem dull, as though I am listening through layers of foam.

Lead has gathered among my eyelashes and it takes a huge effort to force them open. The back of my throat has a scratch I hadn't noticed just hours before. My feet feel disjointed as if they are someone else's warming by the fire. *Am I feverish? My cheeks are hot. Am I just unwinding? Or is this the first nudge of sickness?*

Rain is coming. We must set up the tents, and quick. There are deep violet and green storm clouds gathering and it won't be long until they find us. We run around like ants. Tent bags are thrown from the truck, and we catch them heavily (oof, in the stomach). There is the constant sound of movement, the click-clack of tent poles locking into place. Ant and I are again the last ones, we roll the sleeping bags out in the tent just before the first cloud opens. Quick. Inside.

The first few drops sound heavy on the tent wall – they hit straight and explode quickly, like bullets. In minutes the entire tent is saturated.

We sit inside, head torches flicked off, in the darkness. It feels like our own cave, a place to safely wait.

After an hour, then two, it appears we'll be here for the night. The rain doesn't let up. I peel off clothes and change into pyjamas and hope to get warm. Even tucked underneath layers of clothes and a winter sleeping bag, my body feels frozen.

Ant unzips the front of the tent to peer out. The night air rises inside at once, like a choir standing. A few nibs of chill push into the tent, feeling like early morning frost on our skin. She zips it back up quickly. It's summer, yet chilly. The ground could freeze but, with such a foggy mind, I can't find ways to make sense of this.

My head sweats even though it's the only part of me not wrapped in wool. I wonder if I have Nurofen somewhere, but can't muster the energy to find it. *It would be easier at home.* It's the first time I've had that thought. It would be easier to get more Nurofen. Go to the doctor. Curl up in my bed for days, surrounded by tissues and water, and not have to move. Instead I have scrunched up a cold jumper as a pillow.

Ant, unable to sleep, has sat up, a shawl wrapped around her neck and arms, and is scribbling in her diary. *Is the light too much?* She tries to dim her head torch slightly, but it keeps a steady stream of orange tunneling through the pitch-black night.

When she turns it off, everything goes dark. Outside the clouds gather and the rain lashes our tent sideways. I fall backwards, as one does from a ledge, head first, into the large hands of a strange dream.

**WE RISE** before the sun on little sleep. Everything is saturated. Large concave circles bend each side of our tent like two hands holding puddles of water, big as bowls. One unlucky pair who didn't peg deep enough were propelled towards the graduated hill; which leads, eventually, to the Nile. Their tent tobogganed, stopping only when they were snagged by an overhanging tree branch.

We wring out clothes and water-swollen towels. Nothing has escaped the downpour. We must wear wet shoes, damp socks and sopping jumpers. There are faces of cringe as we squelch our way to the morning fire. It smokes more than usual, and takes a while to catch as wet wood tries to burn.

No-one is amused. At the fire we turn our backs to it, then fronts, rotating like pigs on a spit trying to dry out as much as possible. Anything still wet is stuffed into backpacks with the risk of arriving at the next place smelling like mildew. We eat fire-smoked toast with lashings of butter and it warms us from the inside. Thankfully a dash of hot water, a clump of sugar and the deep, bitter paste of instant coffee soothes immediately.

The morning sun slips her head above the earth, and a thin line of red splits the earth from night. Matilda's chug-chug engine switches over. It shudders like a belly laugh, roaring at us as we drip our way across the soil and climb onboard. Collapsing against seats and each other, we barely mutter more than a hello, and take hours to wake fully.

The landscape changes as we gain metres above sea level, ochre sand turns brown sugar, caramel, the scabby trees with split bark grow coats of moss. Vines layer the hills, adorning them like decorative jewellery, floating in the breeze, crisscrossing each other. Muddy roads.

One of the windows won't close properly and as Matilda picks up speed, the wind howls like a woman in pain. My feet turn cold and blue and, no matter how many pairs of socks I put on, they don't warm until I rub them furiously for twenty minutes. The altitude brings a sharp bite, and we start to layer clothes. Singlets. Thermals. Turtlenecks. Zipped vests. Beanies. Gloves. Extra socks. Ant and I rug up until we are only eyes peering out, which makes us laugh.

What I wouldn't do, she says, for some sun right now. She had just come from Peru, Jordan, Syria, Egypt – she rattles off the list of countries like a shopping list. Six weeks. Blazing heat.

She points out a ring on her left finger. Moonstone and pearl. Carved into the shape of a beetle. A sacred beetle. But after weeks in the Middle East and now Africa it's brown with dust and dirt.

'It's a long time to be away from home,' she says looking out the window at the blue sky. 'When you're only twenty-one.'

When I was twenty-one I left Sydney for the first time and moved to Taiwan. I packed the largest suitcase I could find with clothes that would never be worn in the tropical Taiwanese heat – jumpers and scarves and sneakers and jeans. I sweated through months living there, even in the winter. Humidity sat heavy, and everything around me seemed to ooze.

Back then, I'd only just begun to understand the pull of elsewhere, and yet Ant had been doing this for years.

'If I'm honest,' she whispers in a low voice, 'my heart really isn't in this trip.' She pauses. I wait for her to finish.

'It's at home with my—' she stops for a second. 'Well, I suppose you'd call him my lover.'

Phil was older than she was, but the way she said older I imagined him to be in his fifties, wear tweed jackets and smoke a pipe, but at twenty-seven, he was younger than me. An environmental scientist, he was quiet, she said, selective, preferring woods and water to people.

'We like coffee on Sundays,' she said. 'Dark black and bitter. And we curl up in bed, naked, and sip it and talk. About everything. He has this mind,' she uses her hands to paint a world, a globe, bigger than our faces, 'that thinks about things that other people don't.'

She leans forward, so close our covered noses could touch.

'What about you? Do you have someone?'

I think back to the man I lived with in that damp, ground floor flat. In the first few weeks he declared I was his muse – extraordinary and addictive. I liked the shape of his hands. Good, earthy hands, square palms and muscular fingers from years of living in the country; pulling out trees and working the land. He could fix almost anything around the house, and after dating so many men with soft office hands, pale and slender, I was bewitched.

In hindsight, liking him for his handyman abilities shouldn't have been enough to move in with him. And the way he described me – like heroin – should have been equally unsettling. But, of course, we didn't consider that.

When the passion burnt out, and I lost my way, we turned on each other. How could he not fix me? He could fix everything else – the toaster, the vegie garden, the halogen lights. How damaged we must have been to stay. How broken we were, staring at each other over dinners with empty eyes. Continuing on with our days, living lives that should not have been ours.

*We know, don't we, on some level when we are committing atrocities of the heart?*

So when I think of Phil and Ant snuggled up in the curves of each other, I think merely, that's nice. I'm not jealous. Instead I think, what a relief I don't have someone so close to me, so close they can see inside. And then I wonder how long it has been since I've had a real coffee, and what I wouldn't do for a dark, chuggy espresso that tasted like soil from the earth.

I shake my head.

'Did you?' she asks.

'Not in a long time.'

I see the breadcrumbs of her questions. She thinks I have left behind a lover. A wild passionate affair, scorned, that spun me to the other side of the world. If only it was that, it would be a much easier story to tell than the truth.

And I'm not ready to tell anyone that.

**MATILDA NEEDS** petrol. We stop in a small village with one gas pump, some scraggly trees and a cluster of brick houses. A man is crouched outside one of the houses bent over a camp stove. Two dishevelled dogs are curled on the dust. We stroll over to take a closer clock. A charred black pan perches above the naked flame of a campfire, small wood and coals giving off immense heat; inside are drops of batter: banana and oat pikelets. He's selling them for thirty cents each. We buy them all. Piping hot, we shove them into our mouths. Too hot they burn, leaving a layer of skin that will flap and fall off in a day. But they taste as they smell buttery and golden and crisp delicious. They warm us from the inside out. We are all smiling again saying, 'Did you see how much rain gathered on top of the tents?'

'Incredible!'

I was freezing but now...

How little it takes to turn the day around out here.

Before we leave, the engineers among us pull their wet clothes from their packs, tie them to each other, and anchor them onto a stick they hold out the window.

Nothing makes an entrance quite like Matilda's blue face caked with dirt, her tyres heavy with mud and a multicoloured ribbon of underwear flying through the conservative religious streets of Jinja.

The campsite is lush, green and spacious and stretches about a mile. We construct tents quickly. We know exactly how the poles meet. Where I pull down, when Ant pushes up – the right amount of weight and tussle to get our tent, standing in minutes.

Sarah tells us to take a motorbike, *boda boda,* into town. She points down the campground driveway to a cluster of men who wait at the stone gates with their rusted bikes.

The boda boda man insists he can fit both Ant and I on the back of a bike that wheezes and has rusted springs. I am slightly perturbed by his optimism. Ant swings on first and I slip in behind her. The bike creaks and dips under our weight.

The man lifts his leg, kicks down fast and guns the bike with a putter and a plume of smoke. No helmets. Excitement flutters in my stomach.

The day is bright and warm. Sun filters down through magnificent tall trees. We ride past large houses, estates really, dilapidated, tilting at treacherous angles. There are gaps between houses and blocks where crops were once sown, but now wild plants have taken over. Left to grow and twist together. Broken fences and gates and crumbling tall stone walls are wrapped like presents in ribbons of creeping fuchsia bougainvillea. There are fields growing nothing, grazing nothing. This place has space. *Could I live here?*

We zoom past kids throwing around an empty Coke bottle over a stone wall, seeing who can catch it first. The day smells of ripe mango and freshly cut grass. Feeling more confident, I let my hands go from Ant's waist and spread them wide like a bird. The warm breeze hits them and bounces off me as we zigzag around other bikes.

We attract a fellow boda boda man carrying a large clump of bananas freshly cut from the tree, sap oozing out the end. The fruit, still green, with yellow ripening tips. He waves hello then speeds off around a corner, down a narrow, unpaved laneway with a sheer drop on either side into overgrown plantations.

In town, we're dropped at the corner of the main road. Street signs point to the bank, the grocery store, the town hall, but the rest of the signs state in large black print, *God is Great* with an arrow to the nearest prayer house. Muslim women shuffle past us wearing burkhas and chadours. We feel naked in just cotton tops and shorts.

Further up the road we find a lady selling racks of hand-stitched dresses and skirts. Ant tries on an oversized white slip with blue flowers. She needs to triple in size to fit into anything. I, on the other hand, fit perfectly into a flowing black skirt with pink and red lace flung in bolts at the bottom so it looks like the sun is setting across my calves. For only three dollars, it's a bargain. I buy two and wonder how to keep them from getting dirty.

Next door the local internet kiosk still has dial-up internet. Signs around the shop in bright red warn, *No Pornography*. Some are even taped over the computer screens. The internet, not unusually, isn't working. 'No connect, no connect,' the man keeps saying.

At a roadside cart we browse through locally made jewellery. Dried banana earrings, banana twine rings, even banana-shaped banana string necklaces. If I get hungry could I nibble on a banana anklet?

The shopkeepers, mostly women, sit on fold-out chairs and wooden benches eyeing us curiously. Further down we browse in a thatched jewellery store for ten minutes before a voluptuous lady strolls over to us, her large hips swaying in a multicoloured skirt of chartreuse and mustard silk falling to her calves.

She points to the pair of earrings in Ant's hand. 'From banana.'

Ant holds them up to her ears, 'What do you think?'

'They're lovely,' I say. And they are. The banana twine has been rolled to fine thin columns, which has dried a dark straw colour, almost black in some places, and each column has then been twisted beautifully around itself like a snail shell.

The woman rushes over, filling our hands with banana necklaces, shell bracelets, glossy mint-green seeds strung on leather and zebra-print earrings.

'Look at this,' she says giving me a zebra-print brooch. 'And this.'

Ant gets a handful of wooden beads tied on banana string.

'Or this!' An elephant shaped magnet.

'You are my good friend. You make me happy, I make you happy. I give you good price.'

Up close I can see her coiffured hair, perfectly sprayed and straightened into a beehive standing ten centimetres off her head. A mustard-yellow handkerchief tied tightly around her head comes to two perfect points framing her beehive, like wonderfully exquisite extraterrestrial antlers.

Ant points to a small beaded crocodile. 'How much?'

'Four thousand.'

Indeed. That's two dollars.

'One thousand,' I say boldly.

'Oh friend, no no no, too little.' She answers smiling as we begin the necessary bartering dance. 'Really, how much?'

This goes on for another five minutes. Finally, we agree on 2500 (just over a dollar).

'You are good to me.' She nods slipping the beaded crocodile into a bag for Ant. 'Wish you both good luck.'

At an outdoor market Ant and I find pendants, hearts and globes with wire shells firmly clasping a jewelled crystal inside. Tiger's eye for protection, blue lace agate dug from deep within Namibia and South Africa, and lapus lazuli, a midnight glance streaked with gold flecks. From every angle it looks like a recreation of the universe.

Business is heaving. Everyone wants to touch these beautiful creations, and not one is the same. Ant has struck a firm relationship with moonstone from her days in Jordan and Petra, and she selects a dainty, milky white ring that slides easily onto her right ring finger.

'In flow with the moon, the cycles,' the wise lady with grey hair in a side plait says, her wiry fingers quickly replacing the moonstone gap with a pair of square citrine earrings.

I take my time choosing. Some feel hot in my hand, and others freezing cold. I wonder which one I'm meant to be choosing. Should I just close my eyes and pick one at random? I hold an amethyst up and the dangling pendant catches the November light, splaying it forth tenfold, the rays landing on my chest like a squashed grape.

Ant drifts off towards silks and shawls. She is happy to linger there all day wrapping them around her neck. There's plenty of time to choose.

I see a pendant I hadn't seen before. Was it always there, or did it just appear? The wiry fingered lady is quick. Without the wire casing of the others, it isn't held by a globe or a heart or metal-wired square, but is simply threaded on a silver chain via a small hole in the top of its spherical body. A round, smooth simple stone, with layers of gentle pinks, brown and grays, it looks like a soft winter blanket you'd want to be wrapped up inside when everywhere is raining. Botswana agate.

The lady nods as she watches me touch the other crystals underneath the thin warm pads of her fingers. Lining them up. When I clasp it around my neck it sits warm and light, just above my heart, as though I've always worn it. The lady says, 'That's a stone for healing.' She pauses. 'But mostly a stone of possibility.'

I laugh. Fate seems to have found me, even here, on a dusty street in Jinja. Nothing is by accident, is it?

I show Ant. 'Beautiful!' she exclaims, examining it in the light. She steps back and says, 'It suits you.'

Does it? I'm pleased. I pay for the necklace without bartering. I'd pay any price for something that feels it's always been mine.

As we leave the markets Ant hooks her arm into mine, tilts her head to the blisteringly blue sky and says what fine luck for both of us to find exactly what we needed here. *Yes indeed, what damn fine luck.*

We wave a boda boda down the street, like we live here. We climb aboard with ease, and this one doesn't dip. The breeze feels glorious against our skin, the afternoon sun weakens. Some kids playing by the side of the road, tossing an empty cola can, stop to wave frantically at us. 'Hello!' they shout. We wave back.

The streets are full of palms but emptied of people. The sun hides for a second behind a passing cloud. The wind pauses. After that the whir of the bike is the only sound on the still street.

Back at camp, there is already a haze of voices over the rice and stew dinner. People share photos of their days – some have shopped, some walked, some took a kayak onto the rushing rivers below. Everyone has tales to share. We drink cups of tea. We dunk stale biscuits into them, until they drip with milky heat and we shove them into our mouths before they disintegrate. Everyone falls exhausted into sleeping bags. The smell of toothpaste. The sound of tent zips done up tight.

Later, as I walk around the campsite, the moon barely a thumbnail scratch, crescent and thinning, grey moths flit near the overhead light. Brushing their bodies against the grate, lured by the lip of the light. Petite piebald wagtails glide under tree branches, like low-flying planes. In the near darkness, towards the edge of camp I can make out the soft nightglow of white wings, butterflies busy pattering their flighty feet into the faces of flowers.

**THERE ARE** days like this: it rains and our entire wardrobes, tents, sleeping bags are saturated; the fire won't light properly; we run out of butter or fresh bread, or worse still, coffee; we must pee in a bush of thorns or in the open – still in the rain; someone accidentally smashes a glass of beer on the bus and all day the bus smells stale, like old pubs; we can't sleep at night and counting sheep from 100 backwards doesn't work; we lay there shivering; when the day comes we're still wet.

There are also days like this: clotted cream clouds, sunsets streaking across the sky. Ant and I get the front seat on the bus, 180-degree views, the world opening up to us like a present unwrapped; a zebra stops long enough, close enough, for us to stare in its eyes; we find shade for lunch; we eat cucumbers that have been stored close to chunks of ice and are still crisp; there's a toilet in town; we can get the radio to work and someone links their iPod and the entire bus starts singing, making up words to *The Lion King* songs. We hike in the giant wilderness that has been left to grow as it should; we spot meerkats and a baby giraffe; at night we watch the sunset in silence, all twenty of us, staring in delight as the sky begins her opus; we crawl together in a group, huddled, drinking powdered hot chocolate with boiled milk from the coals, and it tastes like the most expensive drink in the world.

I learn how to say hello in Swahili, (*jambo*). Thank you in Kenya (*asante*) and after we cross the border into Uganda (*weebale*). This is all you need for a quick exchange – buying bananas or a dry top.

I pencil African sayings into the cream pages of my diary. *To get lost is to learn the way. Travelling is learning. Coffee and love taste best when hot.*

And my favourite – *if you think you are too small to make a difference, you haven't spent a night with a mosquito.*

**IN KAMPALA** we feel like ants among giants. I think I know how it feels to be in a city – I come from one after all – but really, I don't. I come from the suburbs on the outer edges. A place of lawns and parks, a place that smells of grass cuttings and roadside freesias, where dogs bark to each other as the sun rises.

Once dropped into the middle of the city, we are devoured by peak hour. People hurry by. Shoulders of strangers collide. They shove and then recoil as if burnt. Heads are down. Bodies rigid as though about to run at each other in rugby tackle formation. Feet march quickly to keep up. The flow. Men yell to each other. Some wheel carts. Cars stop without indicating because drivers want to drop off packages, or pick them up, causing traffic jams where they shouldn't. Stereos boom, speakers are frayed. Heels clack and click on cement.

I feel woozy. Had I once enjoyed this? Had I sought out the pulse and buzz?

We follow everyone on their way to work. Past laundromats. Churches with domed ceilings and large crucifixes. Cafes not yet open. Dusty supermarkets with dim lights, the musty smell of packet soup mix. Parks with no trees. Parks with one tree. Dented cars. Old trucks. Rusted vans. Somewhere the city is squealing with a fire alarm, smog a suffocating blanket of thick haze.

People walk into air-conditioned buildings and, already sweating in the heat, I want to follow them inside. We amble like tourists, and become lost several times. There are street signs and then none. In one area of town all the buildings look the same. The townhouses match each other; identical rusted roofs, front gates painted years ago a creamy white. Now flaking and peeling under the sun. Wooden porches with short awnings. In the winter they would be wonderful places to catch the sun fall in sprees.

We have a map, but I think little of using it. What good can come from following someone else's lines? Find the church. The bridge. The hall. Now go left, now straight, turn right. Can't we just walk? There is something so attractive about turning yourself over to the luck and mystery of this way. Letting the world decide where you should land.

Two fortunate turns and we find a cafe and order espresso. It arrives, a perfect, earthy mix of water and coffee, bitter with a hint of roasted nuts. We order another and shoot it back, like Italians do, before stepping back outside.

It's impossible not to keep moving in this giant tide of people. At a nearby building site men are constructing a new tower. Jack hammers cut through concrete, the clank of cement blocks landing on top of each other. It's almost lunch time and people descend from buildings, ravenous and thirsty. The hustle of people at markets. Bags of groceries. An old dusty computer store.

I'm surprised the familiarity doesn't soothe me but rather, it jars. I'm coming to understand a city always moves. There's so much to see; too much. No matter where I stand – in a cooled shop purchasing a pack of gum, waiting to cross at the lights, even in the park growing wild flowers – I can't feel still.

Had it always been like this in the city? Had I never noticed it when I sat in Sydney's Martin Place to nibble a sandwich, to get some fresh air. When I thought I was relaxing, had a part of me always been churning? Thinking about the next hour, meeting, appointment, deadline. *Had I never stopped even when I thought I had?*

Ant wants to find the fashion district and after wandering for a while, we do. She buys a new top in cerulean blue, silk with a ruffle, incredibly beautiful and impossible to wear on a camping trip. But if anyone can manage it, it's her. At the next store I try on a pair of shorts, crisp white and perfect for summer, but they barely fit. I'm still carrying the weight of Sydney winter and, despite hoping, it hasn't yet melted away.

In five hours we've explored all the streets our tired feet can. We find a park with a large overhanging tree. Men in crisp white business shirts come out for an afternoon stroll. A lady pushes a large blue pram. Some pigeons coo to each other from the top of power poles.

At a small cafe we share a piece of chocolate cake, the layers delicious and moist as though they've been made with double cream instead of milk, chocolate shavings rather than powder.

Before sunset (we'll go home soon), we stroll for a while longer down the streets. They're a nicer place to be without the heat. We find jewellery stores and a place that sells brass taps perfect for bathtubs with claws. An eager man wants us to buy a lamp, but we have no place to plug it in. Even still, he insists it's a great bargain.

When we come out it's almost dark. Perhaps I should be scared, but I'm not. The silhouettes of the city's buildings rise like lumbering giants on the horizon. Cranes turned off mid-swing jut into the air like strange metal arms. The streets hold a sweet smell, the thickness of diesel and jasmine.

The taxi we order doesn't arrive. We wait for an hour, watching the gridlock groan of traffic. Diesel fumes start a headache. My sinuses, blocked, begin to have a pulse. We don't know how to get home. This should scare me too, but it doesn't.

We follow a street on a whim. None of the names sound familiar and that should worry us, but it doesn't either. We meander around the city streets and it's possible we go in circles for a while.

'Are we lost?' Ant finally asks.

'Yes.'

We sit on a curb and share some water. Somewhere in the distance headlights bounce against the road and shine in our eyes before disappearing again.

I had thought being lost would feel like swimming into a dark ocean further than I could stand, my mind fearing the many things that could be lurking below. But I am learning how soothing it can be to encounter the world without knowing what comes next.

We walk past buildings with their lights switched off. Most have gates and some are broken and unhinged. The metal has rusted in places, and as we lean against them to catch our breath, my hands come away with the blood scent of old metal. I keep sniffing them, not sure if I like the smell or not.

We are humbled by the kindness of people who stop and ask if we need help, if we are lost. One man dials a taxi for us – but we'll never know if it comes or not, the city remains at a standstill. We decide it's best to keep moving. At the top of a hill, as if by perfect synchronicity, a stand of taxis sit outside a shopping mall.

On the drive back to our camp, I am full of gratitude. If we hadn't got lost we wouldn't have found the great coffee, the chocolate cake, Ant's new top. The kindness of strangers.

If I hadn't got lost in the first place, I wouldn't be in Africa at all.

**THERE IS** the common notion that love and marriage find you when you least expect it. In Uganda, it finds me in the fruit markets.

In the middle of a large town square, temporary roadside carts have been pulled together. Splintering wooden slabs are transformed into makeshift table tops. The lingering musk of cigarette smoke blows into the African air mixing with the earthy sweat of men hard at work.

Layered crates hold split peas and baby carrots. Lentils are stacked in old potato sacks, ready to be washed and soaked overnight until soft enough to be tossed together with oil and garlic. Pineapples are piled precariously in pyramids – some have fallen off tables and roll loosely on the ground. Mountains of onions. Trays that smell of sticky-sweet peaches ripe with soft pink fuzz are favourites. People line up to buy them by the crateful.

Crisp green beans fresh from the earth, still muddied with soil, are piled into shopping bags and sent home to be plunged into stews and soups. Mottled brown and honey-coloured eggs, packed in torn cartons, are on special. We can buy a whole carton. Boil them until soft. Have them with toast. With avocado. And cracked pepper. My mouth waters. I haven't had eggs or avocado in weeks.

Fresh herbs in pots. Mint leaves. Trays of bonnet peppers. Limes, limes everywhere. Papaya, split down the middle, glowing orange like the sunset. Sackfuls of seasonings. The pungency of spices: soft cilantro, black pepper, fiery chillies waiting to be sliced open. The heat, the heat.

'Oh, bananas!' Ant points at a pile of green, yellow and brown bananas at the first stall.

'Twenty-five for thirty thousand.' The man heaves another bunch of bananas, green and hard, onto the table. It's exorbitant, even by Australian standards. Even though we've learnt the skill of bartering, there will always be a tourist price. What if we lived here, spoke the language, shopped every Saturday – twice during the week? *Could we ever be local?* I'm not sure. We keep walking.

There is something splendid about this market, the tables haphazardly thrown together. No pathway, no clear corridor. Because of this, we meander past every stall, carefully past a pyramid of passionfruit, stepping over wilted lettuce and discarded banana leaves, stopping to bend and inhale the scents from a hefty sack of cinnamon. It smells like spiced donuts. Like Christmas.

A market girl sits slumped on a stool shelling peas, breaking the pods, popping them expertly with one hand. Each pea is expelled with the force of her fingers, sailing inches into the air before arriving on the round plate, tight little green balls. Perfect aim.

We're stopped by a shy-looking man with a large grin. His shaved head cut close to his scalp makes his eyes look even larger; he keeps winking at us with his left one. His name is Amarr, but it takes about six times to properly introduce ourselves because we're sure the first five times he says his name is Emma.

We bargain and barter with Amarr and buy twenty-five bananas for a mere 2500 shillings (about seventy cents). They're greener and harder than the other ones, but they'll be wrapped in foil, sweetened with brown sugar and buried under the coals tonight until they're soft. No-one will notice the difference.

'You want more fruit? Passionfruit? Mango?' He asks.

We can't resist his smile, his deep belly laugh. We buy a bagful of passionfruit, bulging at the top, for two dollars.

'They smell so good,' I say, taking the bag he holds out to me. Like summer and pavlova. I can taste them on a mountain of cream.

'You want pineapple?' He takes a knife in his right hand, throws the pineapple into the air, and as it begins to fall he swings the knife through the air, slicing the pineapple perfectly in two, both edges landing on the table in front of him.

'Taste, taste,' he urges, cutting one half into smaller slices. The sweet scent of summer is on our hands and lips. Sticky and good, it tastes like pineapples used to; the rampant sweetness of sugar, the juice flows over my lips and down my chin. We take two shoved in a small bag.

He wants to give me another piece – straight from his hands to my mouth. He won't let me take it in my hands, and every time I try he pulls away. Finally, I lean forward and let him place the sweet pineapple piece in my mouth. *Is this strange?*

'You want Ugandan husband?' he suggests to the group.

'Sorry, I already have a husband,' Candy says as she flashes her wedding ring.

Ant shakes her head.

'And you?' Amarr looks at me. 'You must have a Ugandan husband!' He claps his hands, delighted.

'Do you have a ring?' Ant yells out.

Everyone's looking at me. 'I have a boyfriend at home.'

*Do I?* He beckons me closer.

'Well, you take this.' He puts another passionfruit into my hand. 'For you. And if you ever want a good husband, you come back to Amarr.'

We wave and call out thank you. We have more than we can carry. I resettle the bag onto my hip like a child. From here I can smell the tropical sugar scent of pineapple. Somewhere in the bag it is already oozing sticky juice through a small escape route near the stem that will coat all of the shells of the passionfruit and make dessert a far stickier affair than anticipated.

Candy stops and turns around, yelling across the market. 'She would marry you, if there's a good price?'

Amarr smiles, nods emphatically, then holds up a dowry in his hands: two pineapples and a bag of lychees.

My African worth.

**LIGHT TOUCHES** the edge of the lake. I lie belly-down on the soft grass and peer through the blades.

I am the right height for a baby warthog, a slithering snake, a tired lioness. Grass tickles my chin while dusk falls around. The lake is dug deep into the earth, a perfect bowl, like a glove curved waiting to catch a ball, a comet. Each side rises steeply, except for ours. Instead of being sheered, like a cliff, it bends along the perfectly globed spine of the earth, curving softly to the water's edge. Plants cluster and thrive along the banks – palm, pine, weed and lily.

You could take a swim now, into the navy inky water. If you're a strong swimmer and things go well, you could easily reach the other side in ten minutes, maybe twenty. I dip a toe in and find it colder than I expected for a lake so close to the equator that basks in the sun all year round. My foot submerged, it goes numb within a minute.

Evening comes on slowly, as if it doesn't want to be there. Tonight marks the equinox; a full moon. The others enjoy long, hot showers – our first. Unroll tents and set up lanterns along the lake's edge. This is five-star camping for us. There are lights! Electricity! Hot water! Although earlier, I mistakenly thought the shower wall was black and only when I reached out to turn on the hot tap, the wall start to move in a frenzy, dividing and collapsing. Quickly, I realized the shower walls were green. And the black cloud moving towards me was a swell of mosquitos. I don't think I am overestimating when I say there could have been a million of them.

I can hear the others in the showers now, every few seconds there is the slap of watery hands on body parts, and the telltale *Ouch*! when you are seconds too late.

In the kitchen, on dinner duty I cut and dice the onions. Tonight I have promised a different meal. We've been here a month and have had enough of stews and broths and rice and wilted spinach.

At home, I cook pasta sauce, stirring the freshly chopped tomatoes on a medium high heat, letting them stew in their own seeds and juices, before adding generous handfuls of my favourite ingredients – chilli, basil and garlic. I've learned that less is more, so I choose fewer ingredients and add more of them. An extra knob of garlic to the sauce makes it taste grittier – like the ground. Using red onion instead of brown lightens the pungency. I don't use recipes, or carefully measured ingredients, I add what I think it needs and I taste often. I make pasta from scratch; flour and eggs and water, and roll it through the old silver pasta maker that clamps onto my bench with a steel jaw.

Italians are famous for their relationship with food. There is nothing, they believe, that can't be cured by a good meal. *Mangia che ti passa* – eat and it will be over. In another life was I Italian?

When in Rome, I ate everything. Everywhere. I couldn't stop. Wild mushroom (funghi) pizza by the slice. Garlic in oil – so simple, so wonderful. Basil ripped from its stems and thrown atop everything. Yes, I will have a side of fried zucchini flowers. Yes, and the baked peppers with basil. Go on then, just one more spoonful of the lemon gelato. And the berry. Yes, I can fit in a coffee too.

Tonight in homage, I make a risotto. I have made it many times using dry white wine (more than advised), stems of rosemary cooking in their own juices, plump fresh peas, peeled garlic buds, slow sautéed mushrooms and oven-baked pumpkin. But I've only ever cooked risotto for eight people at most, and never in a place where I can't find cheese or Arborio rice.

Yet here in Uganda, I'm making a vegetarian risotto for twenty-five meat eaters with old African rice and the only cheese we could find in the local village – a lump of herb cheese, waxy and old. And all of this must be done in large stove vats deeper than the length of my entire arm and balanced precariously on a portable gas stove under a small electric light.

By the light of the large lychee moon I begin to cook. There are no herbs to garnish or flavour, no olive oil to swirl on top. There is a little of the wax cheese left after lunch, which isn't such a bad thing. While no-one is looking I take a little nibble – a mouse bite – and realise with disappointment that it doesn't really taste of anything. I take another bite just to be sure, and find it tastes rather like muted wood smoke.

I pour dry white wine with one hand and cheap canola oil with the other, covering the rice buds that lie like husks in cocoons, waiting to grow and soften. I agitate the vat, allowing the rice to be covered with wine and water so they slip over each other. To agitate the vat takes effort. Both hands need to be wrapped in tea towels on the metal handles. I use my entire body in one complete motion, shaking, to mix the layers of oil, rice and wine.

The rule of risottos is this: each grain must always be covered with liquid but not stirred. Stirring the rice begins breaking the grain apart, making a starchy, gluggy mess. Do not stir risottos – ever. Spoons are only ever needed for eating.

The only vegetables left at the markets were limp capsicum, bags of onions and three carrots. We bought them all. I dice them roughly and throw them into the wet white paste. They fall like coloured confetti.

Garlic bulbs found at the bottom of a milk crate by a man at the markets, only after we pleaded, shed their gossamer skins, jumping into the rice like skydivers without parachutes. More salt. More wine. It smells delicious even though my arms ache.

The table is set under the dark, warm sky. The glow of gaslight lanterns is outshone by the moon, which has spent the last hour steadily rising in the sky until she hangs like a dollop of the coldest, whitest cream in the night sky. Soon she will descend again, becoming burnt butter orange, coming closer to earth to get a better view.

By the time the risotto is ready, everyone is starving. Famished. They have lined up with empty bowls and eager stomachs asking, 'Is it ready yet?'

I'm nervous, but the risotto is a success. Ant finishes first.

'Delicious,' she declares, licking her fork clean.

Shamil goes back for seconds. Then thirds. Even those who claim not to like carbs or risotto, saying it's usually gluggy or tasteless, seem impressed. Sarah, who is a considerable cook, insists I write the recipe for her. Pronto.

They offer to do the washing up, after all, I had cooked, but I insist it won't take long. I shoo them out of the kitchen like naughty mice – for some reason I want to be alone; something has suddenly come over me.

For a while I don't touch anything, just sit at the table and watch the moon. Then I use a fork to dig out the last bits of risotto from the bottom of the vat, those that had been seared by the heat and are brown and crunchy like toast crusts.

After I wash up, I need a tea, and boil the kettle until she sings a high soprano note to the heavens. I shoosh her in case others will hear it and want their own cups filled. While I hug the warm cup to my chest, I nibble biscuits and find a stash of chocolate that has to be eaten also.

I'm not quite sure what has come over me. Perhaps there is still a need to be like the Italians tonight, *Mangia che ti passa.*

Eat until it is over.

**I LEAN** my chin against the wall of the shady arbour long after everyone has gone to sleep. The lake calls me and yet when I reach the edge, something stops me. I don't want to go in.

I watch the moon begin her ballet solo. She glides as if lifted by an invisible partner across the sky. When I was little, I used to watch that same moon from my window. If I pushed back my curtains as far as they would go, from where my head lay on my pink pillow, there she was. Brilliant and whole. Me watching her watching me. I was six and then seven and then ten. Still with a pink bedroom, still tucking a glow worm torch to my chest after the lights were turned out so I could read into the night. Up the carpeted corridor my dad snored so loudly it rattled the walls. Even so, my mum slept quietly.

When I lean over the wooden gazebo, I can't see the bottom. Just an inch deep into the water it turns a nightshade black, and this turbidity makes me wonder what mysteries lie below.

If I watch for long enough, fish come to bite the surface. Their tails flitter, carrying currents of soil and sand. For a second, there are hollow shoots, as though I'd put a giant straw into the water, and it had found the bottom, clearing the muck in its way. It seemed as if the place above and the place below the surface aligned for just a little bit, and I could see everything down there.

When I was young, I swam everywhere I could. In the pool, the ocean baths, my own bath, the sea flat and glassy, the mouths of waves turbid and choppy. If there was water, I was never content until I was in it. I never understood why my parents, who always insisted on having a pool, never used it.

Each summer holiday we spent at our cousins' beach house down the south coast, where the sand gets whiter and the ocean cooler. Perfect conditions for a great white shark riding the cold southerly current.

My parents watched me swim, and boogie board, and body surf the waves, minding the bags, holding the fort while my sister took on the larger waves that crested like towers to the small nine-year-old that I was, and steamed through the cove. One would watch me and the other my sister, but never do I remember seeing either my mother or my father enter the water.

It's only recently that my mum has taken up ocean swimming at the age of seventy-two. When she told me, I didn't know what to think.

'Inside the flags?'

'Sometimes.'

'Inside the shark net?'

'Sometimes.'

Part of me wonderfully admires the youth still blooming in her bones. Time hasn't ravaged her body as it has with so many other parents in their twilight years. Yet, part of me worries. Similar worries to those of a parent, but this notion has nothing to do with chronological age. Rather, worries are always bestowed upon the stronger party in the yoke of a relationship. And for the last decade, that has been me.

It was me who fretted whether my father had done his exercises for his hip replacement, taken his medication, wore sunscreen when he was gardening. Wondered why my mother's blood pressure kept rising and she needed daily pills, what the lump in her mouth was, why her back seemed to bend her over and make her a little old lady, well before I was ready for her to be one.

'When you die,' my dad once told me, 'that's it. That's forever.'

My mum doesn't seem to have an ideology on death, only that it happens. If she thinks any more about it than that, she never tells us.

Our dog Dinah died underneath her favourite fern tree in the backyard. She was missing for days and I kept hoping she'd come bounding in from the horses' paddock up the road covered in manure and smelling like something rotten. My mum found her a few days later. When she picked me up from ballet class, she told me 'Kate, it was just her time.'

Dinah must have known it too, as she crawled into the safe cave of the fern tree. Inside the shrub was a hidey hole, the perfect size for a dog – or a small nine-year-old. It was me that taught her to climb in there and stay hidden from the outside world, surrounded by the gold-green leaves. We played in there, slept in there, my head resting on the soft rise and fall of her belly.

I invited other creatures in there with us: birds with broken wings, little possum babies, and the worst, a three-legged cat who couldn't use his limbs after a run in with a car. I tried to save them. Dinah had watched as I tried, many times, to whisper to them, to softly touch fur bellies and wings, and nurse them back to health. I placed them in shoeboxes with old towels in the shape of pillows and blankets. For hours I patted them, and whispered in their ears. I thought that if they were going to live, touch was the way to return, as though my hands held the secrets of healing. And if not, I wanted them to leave the world knowing they weren't alone.

None of them made it.

My mum and dad dug shallow graves and I placed them inside, marking the soil with my tears and making each of us say something. Even now I can't pass an animal on the side of the road without stopping the car and giving it some kind of burial. Even if it is just the crossing of a stick over its soft crumpled body, the laying of a flower. And a quick prayer; *I hope you are in some place better.*

My parents don't know this, but every night I lie in bed and worry one of them won't wake. I dread the phone call that will inevitably come, tear my heart from my bones and mangle it like a soft body in a shark's mouth, ripped and torn, until I can't be put back together again.

*Dear God,* I press these words into the sky at night, *please let them be here tomorrow.* I leave it hanging, a blanket of whispered prayers, pinned to the night sky with stars.

The waterweed churns at my feet. There remains an unease in my stomach; something I can't place. *Have I eaten too much?* I slip off my shoes and stand on the banks of the black sand. The moon reflects off the lake like it's a glistening black hump of a whale, surfacing.

As the waves chop and clap against each other, the lunar pull creates a tide and memories of the past seem to churn again.

I watch the night sky, the moon, and wonder how many times I have watched this same sky from another place across the world.

A Tuesday night, just a few months ago, in Sydney. I was home after dark, boiling water for peas. I flicked on my phone, trawled the latest news, checked my inbox, Facebook. At the top of my feed an old friend had posted some news. Cancer.

This was not *I hope I'm okay, could be out of the woods, remission, some chemo.* No, let's be clear – she was dying.

Comments ensued. *Stay strong, be positive, we love you.* After I read her news, I felt an urge to go outside. I lay on the bare concrete of my backyard, before the grass starts, where the garden table should be. But the table was propped against the garage wall, the caramel glaze drying, waiting for another lick of veneer. I wondered how many more skies she would see, how many more stars, before she didn't.

Before I came to Africa, so many people had lost their grip on the world. There was a particular time, two months, that were steeped in death – friends of friends, slipping away. And then a very close friend of mine, Trevor.

He died in the way you hope everyone goes, and then no-one at all. Three years was long enough – you had time to say a million goodbyes. But because it was that long, and we were wishing otherwise, no-one ever really said goodbye at all.

He was sick. And then better for a while. Then sick again. *Give him a few weeks*, I thought, *another round of chemo, he'll feel better*. I'll pop by just like I always do, and he'll be sitting on the couch, the fifty-inch plasma on mute playing silent video clips, and we'll pull out the nerf guns. His wife Polly will be making us coffee, and we'll be laughing like idiots, all three of us, at life, at each other. I'll only mean to stay an hour, but it always ends up being two or three. Beers would be served just past midday. Whiskey by 2 pm.

When I heard he was sick again, I prayed for miracles, but even as I did, I realised I'd known all along that he was slipping away.

Days later I received a text from Polly in the early ashy dawn of a Tuesday: *His breathing is short. He doesn't have long. Come now.*

I raced around the house trying to find clothes and throw them on in a fury. I caught a taxi by the station then screamed at the cab driver who was in the slow lane.

'DRIVE FASTER! GOD DAMN IT, HURRY UP!'

I remember seeing the sun rise a soft pink over the Lane Cove river and thinking, *it is too lovely a day to be someone's last.*

At the hospital, I ran to the lift, pressing the button to level 7, telling myself to *Breathe, breathe.* The lift was empty, but if anyone had been listening they would have heard me whisper, *Please let me keep it together.* And then, just in case, I pressed my hands together like a prayer, trying to squeeze the sadness between my hands, trying to keep it contained. But it oozed out through the gaps in my fingers, and my eyes were filled with tears before I even reached his room.

*Give me gloves,* I thought. *A blanket, cover me, layer upon layer. I no longer want to feel.*

When I saw him in the room his body wasn't his, his face wasn't his. Instead a baby's body lay before me, skeletal and fragile. His head was a skull with a stretch of white skin, the raspiness of chest wheeze. He slept the entire time, with his eyes open. I don't think he was there anymore.

Polly sat on one side, and I on the other, holding his hands, so warm to touch. I said nothing, but in my mind I told him, *I love you. I know you'd hate that I was being so soppy. But then I know you'd secretively love it too.*

When I said those words silently I watched his face. I felt to see if his hand grabbed at mine. But nothing registered that he had heard anything at all; perhaps he had already drifted somewhere else.

I said goodbye and as I left I cried like a baby. I couldn't be seen like that so I stopped in the disabled toilet and put make-up over the mascara smudges. And when I looked in the mirror I couldn't find myself.

Some hours later, just after midday, he stopped breathing.

On the day of his funeral I wept quietly at the back. The music played and photos of him, flashed on the TV in front of an audience so big we didn't fit inside the chapel. People were sprawled outside some twenty steps away, maybe more.

At the end of the service the curtains pulled together, cloaking the coffin. Although he was already long gone, this act seemed so final.

The sun shined all day, and afterwards, everyone said, 'What a lovely service.'

I kept repeating to myself words from *The lost hotels of Paris* by Jack Gilbert; two lines in particular:

*But it's the having*

*not the keeping that is the treasure.*

For weeks afterward I kept staring at the night sky and asking, *Where are you?*

When I saw traffic and blue skies at lunchtime during my walks around the city, I often went in circles. I asked, *Can you still see us?* I wanted to ask people, do you think he can see? But it was a different kind of question. One that you weren't supposed to admit you thought about. You stuck to the safe topics, like how funny he was, how caring.

Most of the time I thought about things I couldn't talk about. Did he have time before he slipped away to think about his life? And if he did, was it what he wanted? How did he know if it was a good life, how could it be measured? In love? Smiles? Months? Hours?

They kept me up at night; the questions. I'd stare at the ceiling and ask silently, *What did it mean to be not here? In this world, on this earth?* Which made way for other questions, *What did it mean to be here?*

At that vague time of night, answers were never ready and waiting. They stayed in the shadows, cool and damp. They preferred it there. So, of course, lying there desperate, my head full of questions, I couldn't answer any of them.

Some nights I thought I was going mad.

It made me think of Virginia Woolf, who wrote most of her life – when she wasn't stashed away in an asylum for being mad – before finding her end at a river. After several major breakdowns, she feared she had begun to hear voices. I wonder if she suddenly thought, yes, dear life, that is all. Because shortly after she began to hear those voices, she simply stopped eating. By the time she took herself to the edge of the river Ouse to die, she was but a boned woman, with a hanging of skin.

Did she take any last-minute thoughts with her, unwritten ones? Did she count the last seconds of her life in her head – one, two, three. Or did she count backwards, as she stepped deeper, knowing we can only last underwater for two minutes at most, before the water rushes in.

Did Sylvia Plath consider it too, those questions? Perhaps while chopping onions, or organising herb stems in deep troughs of water and letting them drink. Did she read something? Or realise something? Or did she just long for black silence before deciding that all the thoughts she had ever had – would ever have – had already tumbled from her head onto the page and there couldn't possibly be another.

Perhaps she just couldn't bare the strange idylls of life, the crests, the troughs, and out there was an idyllic place where she could rest, if only for a little while. So she plunged her head, whole, into an oven. She didn't light the fire, but instead inhaled the gas and let it balloon her lungs and float her above the world, far, far away from any place that looked like a kitchen.

Did these women sense there was an ending? Did they plan it for weeks, quietly wondering how, or when? Or on a whim of desire, did they both just think now, now, NOW. I must go. And out they left, just like one slips out the back door, before anyone can notice.

My friend Justin decided not to wait out the years, and ravage of nature, that would slowly undo his wide country shoulders, his brazen physique, his large smile.

Just days before he left for a New York summer he told me, 'You got to do it, Kate. Get out there, into life. You gotta do it.'

He was laughing when he said it, and there was a sense of wonder that surrounded him. A desire to experience it all.

A few weeks later, Justin flung himself from an open window, three stories up, onto a Manhattan pavement.

For many months he lay in a hospital bed with dim eyes, repairing broken bones, crushed femurs and shattered wrists. Everyone wanted to know afterwards if, during his many days in rehabilitation, he'd had a moment of insight, a vision, which they hoped would make him want to stay in the world.

But he didn't want to stay. He had stepped into a foggy land and over there felt very distant. He was alone, and no matter what he did, he kept saying he couldn't find his way back. I sometimes wonder if he already had one foot in this world and the other in the next.

Five years later he didn't die of a disease where we had time to whisper, 'I love you,' or watch him dissolve in front of us. Is that better or worse? I don't know.

He left suddenly. Yanked from this life, not by God or anyone else's hand, but by his own. With care, he wrapped the sheets of his hospital bed into a circle that looked rather like the twisted colours – blue and white – of an inflatable life buoy. And then, just as if he was lost in the water, he reached out and slipped his head through the float. And he was pulled swiftly into another world.

After he left, I spent night after night staring at the sky. I couldn't fathom the thought that my friend had simply vanished. We were no longer lit by the same moon. His sky wasn't mine. He was no longer here. And no matter where I went, or how long I searched, I would not find him.

There is some mysterious process at work here, the continuous chime of life, the bell tower counting out our life – how many rings are left? Did Justin use up all his rings? Or did he just climb that bell tower and cut the ropes and stop the world measuring another moment.

Oh time, there you are, marking us – beginnings, middles, ends – a sly little measurement that builds parentheses around our life, and we must live within it.

Do you know that in some places, Lake Bunyonyi is said to be over 900 metres deep? So deep, no-one actually knows how far it goes. I think about getting in. Just swimming out. There are no sharks. No snakes. Possibly an eel. Just water and depths of it. There is really nothing to be afraid of.

Except dying.

I keep wondering what it feels like to die. To leave. Do we know it when it's happening? Do we have a sense of it? Does it make us feel sick and woozy, losing a body? Or light and floaty, like gaining feathers? The thought makes me a little dizzy. I try my mantra. *I'm fine. I'm fine. I'm fine.*

But when I breathe, when I stop thinking about how fine I am, something dark rushes in. I try not to think it, but I can't stop. I wonder if everyone has a longing for a place that isn't here. I wonder if, like me, they understand Justin and Sylvia and Virginia – just a little too well.

**THE SUN** rises slowly over the coconut plantations of Rwanda. Banana trees. Empty lots and vacant houses. Fields of palms. Our minivan has been climbing since before dawn. We are up but our faces are still smeared with sleep, eyes that opened before they needed to, faces puffy.

The locals have risen early too. There seem to be hundreds of them, all heading in the same direction – to the plantations. Each carrying small crumpled paper brown bags with lunch. Plain ugali. A piece of coconut. A soft brown banana.

A lucky few have bicycles. They meander carefully in-between the walkers. Our van slows to a crawl. A light mist hangs in the cool morning air. Fog billows.

At first light, we begin our walk. Rudi, our guide, does a sharp right, leading us between a line of irregular mud huts. We step carefully, taking care to avoid a line of baby-green cabbages. Budded heads poke through the soil.

Someone has gathered new potatoes from the ground, perhaps only this morning, and they sit in a wicker basket under a clothes line, white like luminous eggs, with a light dusting of dirt.

Just beyond the last cabbage head, chickens are squawking and strutting under a line of wet washing hung on string. The closer we get to the hens the louder they crescendo. *Are they welcoming us? Or protecting their yard?* Either way, African chickens are loud. The noise they make is astounding.

Beyond the chickens and washing, someone had taken the time to lay the earth in perfect rows. Overturned with precision, the soil heaved and turned, black and damp, waiting for seeds. Worms wriggle with translucent pink skins. Digging holes back into the black earth so their nude skin won't be scorched by the sun.

We are all so busy peering down and watching the worms that we don't realise Rudi has stopped. A man of little words, he merely puts up a hand, no words, asking us to pause. And when we do, we look up, and get our first real look at the Sabyinyo mountain.

She is as overgrown and beautiful as I imagine that garden in the Bible. So tall, she crescendos from the earth, accompanied, I imagine, by an orchestra. The clash of cymbals, the deep boomed tuba, the peal of a French horn, the triumphant streams of many trumpets. The top of her is completely obscured by cloud and mist. (An eerie oboe hangs on long after the brass instruments have ceased.)

Behind the mist, instead of a peak at her head like most volcanoes, she has a cone, shaped over many years, heaving lava at the sky. Sabyinyo means tooth, and on days the clouds part, the top of her is said to resemble the retracted gums of an old man, smiling upon Rwanda.

Crossing the fields the farmland ends suddenly, giving way to a long stone wall. At one end – you could easily miss it – a small archway formed entirely of plants and wildflowers. The opening, bordered by tiny pink flowers and thick vines is narrow, like a machete has cleaved an entrance weeks ago and it has grown back steadily since. We have to duck to enter the Sabyinyo, like one does when entering a cave.

Plants, vines, thorns, twigs, trunks so large three of us joining hands can't wrap our arms around it. The sun is not allowed in here. Gallium vines have climbed the trunks, skyward, like a race to the sun. Those that did not hitch rides have spread sideways instead, layering the ground like knotted hair. Beneath the latticework, the soil is as dark and syrupy as molasses or a morning brew of roasted coffee.

There is a strange springy feel to the ground below our feet. Ant and I jump. Once. Twice. Laughing – it feels like we're bouncing on a trampoline. Below our feet lie ancient rotting tree trunks, covered in lime and jade moss. Together they pad the ground, softer than any mattress I know. The other guide Jonste notices us and says the flooring means we can fall without hurting ourselves. *Thank goodness*, I think. Then I wonder, *Where would I fall from?*

I bend down and feel the exposed roots of a eucalypt. Cool to touch. So different to the heat of their trunks in Australia. Moving my hand up the root, pressing again as though I were checking a leg for a bone break. The moss and soil, soft and spongy, I kneel without any discomfort, and stay there looking up at the tree as though I have come to pray at this cathedral of cover. When the breeze blows, green and gold leaf litter flitters from branches like soft-bodied moths, coming to rest on the ground.

A scent of dampness rises when we move and a sweet rotting; ancient jungle soil. There are no paths. Plants have grown across every inch of light and space. Matted nests of vines and prickles. We stand silently in a group staring at the tapestry of leaves and trunks. Life has covered everything in sight. *Where do we begin?*

Rudi pulls at a small hole in the vines that crisscross at eye level like thick, sinewy spider webs. Drawing his machete, he warns us with a quick flick of his left hand: stay back. He swings once, twice, slashing at air first then finding plants. Vines melt to the ground. Small trees waver.

We follow Rudi along the narrow path, so tiny we must walk with our hips and shoulders turned sideways. Twisting our bodies to fit through. Prickly plants reach for us, waiting to sting. One swipe, even a touch and the skin burns like a thousand mosquito bites. When I forget to twist or lose my balance – which happens several times – I'm stung fiercely. Tiny red bumps appear immediately. I don't know if I'm meant to be scratching the poison tips out, or licking them with the mild anesthetic hidden in my saliva. The bumps rise in angry welts. I'm even stung through my jacket.

A break appears in the canopy and the sun pours down, making everything golden. Flowers flourish, tiny white bud heads. Fragrance fills the whole hillside. Rudi continues to sway his machete like he's conducting an orchestra.

Deeper into the heart of the jungle, flowers disappear into different shades of green – olive, bottle green, mossy, lime, deep sea green. Vines so matted they cling to rocky walls, creating thick latticework. Ledges and platforms made entirely of vine.

One type of vine looks like a thin green tree python. Winding itself around the tall forest tree trunks, it seems intent on strangling them. The other, brown and long like a stick, sinewy to the touch, could bend and bend and never break. It hangs off the trees, a loopy tentacle catching in our hair and grazing our faces like alien fingers.

Rudi stops, hand up, and we pause behind him. He flicks his hand towards the vine, and again points up. *We are going to climb it.*

It's just vine attached to rock. It has been there for hundreds of years, and offers footholds and finger reaches. From down here, it seems more like one of those childhood nets you'd climb in the playground.

Except if I fell from them, the drop was only ever a metre and into the soft grass or chipped bark plentifully dropped below. Here, we will have to climb to the first ledge, which is at least double my height. And if you fall, there are a lot of things that will catch you – the ragged ends of trunks, and tall bamboo stems waiting to impale. If you avoid these, there's nowhere to go but the bottom of the cliff, below us, covered in smooth grey rock.

The way to climb plants is an art form, unquestionably settled deep in the genes of Rudi and Jonste. Rudi lifts himself up the vine with ease, as though going up stairs. Ant and Candy and Bazz follow one by one with a little more effort, groaning slightly as they pull their body weight up, tufts of slippy vine in their hands. Still they work it like able rock climbers.

My turn. The vines creak as I place my right foot carefully in the thickest place and grab somewhere above me. My hands sweat and they slip off the first vine. I reach again and grab another vine with more grip. But it seems I've placed my leg too high and now it just looks like I'm doing a very deep stretch for my left hip and groin. Repositioning my leg a little lower, I heave myself upwards with a loud grunt.

*Where do I go next?* My right foot is wavering about and I know I must put it somewhere, but suddenly there doesn't seem to be any more footholds. The vines look like sluiced grasses on a wet day, and my foot will just slide right off. I'm stuck. I hear a creak and start to panic. *Is the vine breaking?*

All politeness forgotten, Jonste places both his hands on my rear and pushes me up from behind. Rudi leans over and reaches for my left arm. Sturdy as he is, he uses every ounce of muscle power to pull me up by my hand. My fingers feel as if they could dislocate at any moment. I gasp, red-faced.

And then suddenly I am up and the vines are holding us all at the top, on a flat surface about a metre deep, as easily as a rock ledge would.

'I don't dare jump on these ones,' I tell Ant.

She smiles at me before doing a little jump. I lean out to the wall of vines and grab hold of them.

With the vines below, and the jungle spreading in front of us, the view is quite stunning. But we can't stop here. 'There is much more to go,' Rudi says.

We plod upwards, back on terra firma thank goodness, sticking in mud and undergrowth and leaning on the vines that hang from tree boughs when we need to breathe. The air seems thinner now. We fill our lungs but little air rushes in. I'd always imagined jungle forests to lay low to the earth and sea level, and mountains with high altitudes to be covered in Alpine fir trees and snow (even in summer).

Us Australians seem to be struggling the most to find our breath out here. I suppose it's not a surprise given the relative flatness of our country and how most of us live on or near the coast, with only gentle slopes to roll down to the beach. The tallest mountain we boast, Mt Kosciuszko, wouldn't even rate as a hill here. In fact, the top of Kosciuszko is closer to sea level than the farmland we first walked through to reach the Sabyinyo.

Rudi machetes a new pathway. I squeeze my shoulders in so as not to touch more prickly plants. Two get me. They burn, a hot sting that makes me want to slap my skin for a full minute. We climb upwards, the mist grows, and everything feels cool and moist.

We climb more vines. I'm hanging onto my camera with one hand and a very thin vine with the other, jutting off the rock at a strange angle like I'm about to abseil back down it. You think I'd know what to do by now – we've been trekking for at least three hours – but I have little energy left to haul myself up. Jonste assumes the push position and Rudi pulls again. Finally, I'm up. Rudi clicks his tongue once against his teeth and nods. A silent thumbs-up. We have their scent.

At the top of the next incline he stops abruptly, sending a few people into his back. He points ahead: a tuft of black fur. Moving. Slowly. A human hand with fur reaches up out of the grass and grabs a branch. The familiar sound of snacking, like someone slowly munching on a large stick of celery.

Gorillas.

The black head turns. Two eyes stare directly at us. Wide, beautiful eyes. His nostrils flare with each breath. He smells of jungle and sweat – *or is that us?* We watch him watching us.

He sits up quickly, crosses his legs like a flexible yoga teacher and reaches for a piece of wild bamboo, ripping it off a tree and holding it aloft for a few seconds like a sword, a call to battle.

He opens his mouth so wide we can see glints of milky calcium teeth. The bamboo disappears quickly inside, and again the sound of munching. When finished, he rolls onto his back, and lets out a grunt as the air escapes him. Distinctly human.

It's a photo frenzy of lenses, zooms and continuous shooting. I'm amazed the gorillas seem unperturbed by a dozen white people clicking at them like demanding paparazzi. Photos of little baby hands picking up bamboo. Click. The back side of the silverback vanishing under leaves. Click. An adolescent climbing quickly in the trees. Click. A gorilla aunt staring straight at us. Click click.

We move to sit in front of a sedate mother and her young baby almost a year old. We watch them eat. The baby eats and plays and climbs, then eats some more. Pulling at grass with hands that look similar to yours or mine. After snack time, the baby runs up a nearby tree trunk then drops onto his mother's head, over and over, which he finds hilarious. She seems, as mothers do, to be used to this bopping of her head.

At times the gorillas talk in muted grunts to each other, which the guides interpret. Before we started the trek, Rudi taught us how to grunt *Hello* in gorilla. Just in case the silverback came at us, thinking we were enemies, or the tribe felt fearful and we needed to do our best to calm them.

The young male juveniles pound their chest several times, which Rudi whispers, as well as saying hello, is their way of keeping warm. They fart many times too, but after being on a confined truck with boys, this is neither surprising nor a revelation.

It's hard to locate the silverback, the patriarch of the family, in the dense undergrowth. We're told to keep ten metres away at all times, especially around him. They're territorial and the protectors of their family. Rudi points. He's found him.

We climb under tough branches and swing out over short crevasses exposing our bodies to a possible freefall into nettles and vines to get closer. Closer still. The silvery coarseness shines in the light reaching a pointed V at the lower lumbar of his back. He's munching on greens and wild celery.

Our cameras are poised. Our breaths held. I drop my camera quietly to my side and cap the lens, preferring to watch in real time.

Jonste leans over quietly and unhooks the camera from my shoulder. 'I carry,' he whispers and pushes me forward, putting his hand on my lower back, guiding me to a better viewpoint.

Someone gets too close. A branch is knocked. Leaves rattle. Does a flash go off? We were specifically told no flashes.

The silverback stands. A mountain of muscle. His chest enlarged, no-one moves. We stand stony as statues. He drops to all fours and with the force of a truck, lumbers quickly past our group. So close to Ant his breath snort tosses her fringe in the air. Quickly, he slips between some trees and vanishes.

Rudi points to his watch. Jonste nods. Our short time with them is already up. We begin the three-hour return journey through the jungle.

Arriving back at the base we're sweaty, dirty, tired and immeasurably hungry. We devour the cheese sandwiches and apples from the guides, munching like the gorillas beneath the shade of trees.

We've been up since dawn, so it's no wonder that as soon as I'm back in our minivan, I sleep the entire way back to Lake Bunyonyi.

I dream of a place without maps. And even so, finding my way.

**I WAKE** unsettled back at Lake Bunyonyi. I hadn't dreamt of anything at all but when I wake, just before the alarm, something feels off. Amiss. Strange.

The alarm clock reverberates against the tent and pounds my head like a gong. Before I even unzip my sleeping bag the cold eats at my bones and makes my knees creak. The alarm goes off again, reminding, punctuating, striking.

Lake Bunyoni is pitch black at 4.30 in the morning. The dock creaks somewhere in the inky blackness and the lake's tide brushes the sand in rhythmic strokes. We throw backpacks into Matilda's belly and our own bodies, still soft with sleep, huddle under open sleeping bags on the faded seats.

It's not even dawn and too cold for hellos. There are many miles to cover today – our longest route of the entire trip. There's no time to even stop for breakfast. Matilda jerks quickly out of the camp. Her wheels sliding on the muddy banks and the unmarked roads out of town.

Everyone dozes except for me. *Have I forgotten something?* I mentally check everything – toothbrush, clothes, backpack, tent. Yes, all stowed below. Diary, head torch, pens, iPod. Yes. The world whips by below. We reach a corner and the driver slams on the brakes. We take it too fast, like a rally car.

Pip is jolted awake. She leans towards the window and watches what I am watching – outside is a blur. We must be doing at least a hundred. Another corner. Why aren't we slowing down? We look at each other and without words I know we're thinking the same thing. Too fast. I pull the doona over my head, blocking out the views, and try to sleep. *We're going too fast.* A gnawing in my stomach.

There is nothing I can do so I cross my fingers, and my legs and my toes, and just hope we get where we are going safely. I hope my prayers will make a difference.

I doze, and when I wake the sun is almost up. There is something about the light that makes things less scary. Pip smiles at me.

We start to unload the food at the back of the truck for breakfast. Bruised apples are passed out. Stale bread that needs lashings of butter to be edible, and even then, it's still rock hard. Shamil grabs the knives, walks down the aisle, handing out.

We bump over a pot hole in the road. We jar and shudder. Simon hits the brakes. Some grab onto seat armrests like we're going through strong turbulence in a plane. It's over as quickly as it began and we smile at each other. Shake it off. It was just a pot hole, after all.

Shamil hands me a knife. And then, seconds later, Matilda loses her grip on the Ugandan roads and starts to slide out of control.

**CAN YOU** feel something is off in the air? Do we know when something terrible is about to happen? When I was sixteen I changed schools, and the only person who befriended me was a strange, red-haired boy called Toby. He was loud, but sensitive. I watched him at lunch and everyone pretended to like him, but no-one actually did. They laughed at him. I'm not sure he ever realised.

In English class, he asked what I was doing one weekend and if I wanted to go for a bike ride or a walk. Craving new friends, I said yes. But as soon as the words were out of my mouth I had friendship remorse, the cruel kind that teenagers often have. *Would people find out? Would I become a social pariah too?*

I started to think how I could get out of it, but the lies just wouldn't come out of my mouth. Instead I began to wonder if perhaps he would change his mind, but he wouldn't, so I thought instead about him not being able to come – a cold, the flu, a sprained ankle. Every chance I had, I imagined him lying in bed too sick to move.

Saturday morning came and I woke with a sense of dread. It was raining. And cold. I couldn't eat. Something was off. When midday came and went and Toby didn't arrive, I felt strange. As though too many thoughts had appeared in my head at once and like helium, they had the power to lift me into the air. I could no longer feel the ground.

When the phone rang, it struck through the silence like a gong. Toby's mum. There had been an accident. In the rain, Toby had spun off his bike and crashed. He had lacerations and gashes, and places where the bone had broken through skin and needed to be pushed back into place. All that morning, I had felt something was wrong. And afterwards, with childish guilt, I worried that I had somehow caused it.

I was thinking about all of this, and Matilda was still sliding.

**IN ENMORE** I rented a house, a townhouse, long and narrow, connected by brick on both sides to identical townhouses, each with the same red door and white window frames I called home. Enmore lies in Sydney's inner west directly under international and domestic flight paths, and the first sound of morning, before the sun arose, was of each individual window pane shaking and rattling as if in an earthquake.

If I'd stood outside on the small strip of grass and a side bed of wood chips that the real estate agent called a manicured garden, I could have reached up and almost grazed the bellies of those metal birds with my fingertips. We were so close, I could count the nuts and bolts fastening the engines to the underside wings. But it was the sound that jarred the most, a whining of metal as the wheels unfolded, a metal on metal grind that seemed to cover the row of townhouses in invisible sound soot.

It is the same sound, metal on metal, that screeches now from the underbelly of Matilda as we fly about inside her berth like the souls in Dante's hell, without place or root or record.

Something in Matilda buckles. Her engines wheeze and she almost gives way, snapping in the middle. Whining like a hurt dog, under the pressure, we jerk suddenly. I drop my apple. Buttered rolls are going flying. We lurch again. *Are we up on two wheels?* Everyone is flung about. Tiff's head makes the sound of a broken egg shell as it cracks into Matilda's metal roof. When the brakes finally kick in, we skid to a stop. Tiff holds her head, whimpers slightly, and when she needs to catch her breath, she holds it, and we all sit there silent, in shock as you do after an accident. Shamil is lying in the middle aisle still carrying – of all things – a bunch of knives ready for breakfast. He is face down and not moving.

Sheer terror makes my heart pump. *This can't be happening.*

We take seconds, or is it minutes, to know what has happened. We have crashed. Or hit something. Or something has hit us.

Sarah frantically bangs on the outside door to our berth. 'Are you okay?'

Someone with a dazed voice – God, I think it's me – shouts hoarsely, 'Yes.'

'Simon's not okay.' We hear the waiver in her voice. 'I'll be back.'

We are locked inside. The only key to our door is tied around Sarah's wrist, and she has quickly disappeared into a stranger's mud cottage a hundred metres up the road. She has no mobile reception, and no-one else can drive us. *Are we stuck here?* It could take days for a new driver to reach us. To find us.

It's humid, hot. The windows fog quickly. Shamil, thankfully with no knife scratches, has stood up shakily and, like a good doctor, is holding Tiff's head, on top of her hands, as though they are both trying to keep pieces of her head together. I wish someone had their hands on my head keeping my pieces together.

Men from the nearby town have started to gather outside, they're banging on the doors.

We stop moving. Perhaps they can't see us? Thankfully, the windows where we have rubbed them to get a better view have fogged over. Behind steamed windows the men look like silhouettes, shadows.

They all look the same. They grow restless and irate, some walk in dusty circles, kicking at stones, talking rapidly on mobile phones. Soon there are more of them; they're calling friends. Then friends of friends.

Sarah makes a dash to the front cabin, and locks herself and Simon, with his limp back, tightly inside. We sit there going nowhere. Matilda groans as the heat of the day emerges.

I find Ant's hand and hold it. Sweaty palms. Both of us. We gulp for air, our chins lifted to the ceiling as we drown in steam, only now and then the wind compassionately blowing through the propped-open sky roof.

*Dear Lord,* I pray, *please please let us be okay.*

Sarah rings through the walkie-talkie phone from her cabin to ours. Cheryl, a quiet Canadian, picks it up. Sarah's voice bounces around the cabin, crackling and tight. 'I don't know what to do.'

Tour guide Sarah has been replaced by human Sarah. No-one knows how to answer her. The men below circle Matilda like dust sharks. Mobile phones keep ringing and they keep answering and talking words we can't decipher. Jerry, Cheryl's husband, takes the phone from Cheryl. I hear then, the most joyous words of that trip. 'I'll do it. I'll drive her.'

'Can you drive trucks?' Sarah sounds nervous.

'That's what I do back home. I'm a truck driver,' comes the solid, stoic response.

Silently, Jerry climbs out the left side of Matilda and carefully into the cabin below, the men with machetes gathered on the right, too angry to notice. He picks his way carefully over Simon's broken back. We pause. Will Matilda start? The engine turns over. Once. Twice. Without catching. A small rumble. Silence.

On the third go, the engine catches. Relief. Matilda groans loudly as Jerry shifts her into gear. Tyres grip. We roll. And shudder. Stop. Jerry brakes. Back to first gear.

The men assemble and watch us with their hands still slightly raised. Anyone watching from afar would think they were ceremoniously waving us goodbye. Matilda restarts, stutters back onto the road as Jerry gets used to the gears. We travel the entire length of the highway, for four hours, never going above second gear.

**WE ARRIVE** in Kenya much later than planned. The campsite is empty. Dusk is settling. No-one is hungry.

A few people skulk about smoking. Some swear and toss about blame – Simon's driving and bad roads.

'No road signs,' they say. The culprit is finally named: unmarked speed bumps. Three of them in a row we encountered going over a hundred kilometres an hour.

Some are mad. Some cry. We'll have to wait for a new truck, and a new driver, before we can enter Tanzania. I eat dry crackers. Everyone has stopped talking. We're all silent. No-one knows how to fill the spaces. Ant makes me a tea later, before bed, and even though it's a hot and sticky night, I drink it. We put up tents in silence and crawl inside.

'What are we going to do?' Ant asks in a small voice from the other side of the tent. She seems like she could be on the other side of the world. 'Do we keep going?'

My mind whirls with thoughts. *I'm scared. Let's go home. Why don't we wear seat belts? The roads here are too dangerous. God, it could have been worse. What if we had rolled the truck? This whole trip could end in disaster. I* COULD DIE HERE.

Lying in the tent, I wait for noises to comfort us. But there is no traffic at this time of night, no birds calling to each other, no murmurs from the other campers. There is no sense of life outside the walls of our tent at all.

Suddenly, a gust of wind arises from nowhere, pushing the trees against the tent. We listen in silence as the leafless branches, stubs, scratch at the roof of our home. Like skeletal fingers trying to find a way in.

I don't say aloud the words I am thinking: *Quit. Go home. Take a plane tomorrow.*

It would be so easy.

**IN TAIWAN,** someone made the grave mistake of allowing me on a scooter under the ill-conceived notion that the faster you went the easier it was to keep balance. Go fast, go straight. Why does everyone want to go in a line? I swung my leg over the bike, placed my hands on the accelerator, pulled the throttle, lurched forward abruptly, a large bunny hop.

'A bit jumpy isn't it?' I said to the spectators.

I turned back, pushed my helmet down further, repositioned my hands. Brake off. Throttle on. I sped up, too quickly, lurching forward. The momentum made my hands jerk and I must have twigged the bars, because I turned suddenly, veering 180 degrees, off the road. Running straight into a parked car.

In Obertsdorf high in the Bavarian Alps, I was convinced the fresh mountain air, and the city's passion for two-wheeled transport, could help me ride. As if by osmosis, biking would somehow permeate my body. In stumbling German I managed to hire a bike for a day, from a rounded woman with grey hair and a plump bratwurst stomach. *Ich mochte ein fahre rad fur ein tag bitte.*

She seemed perturbed that I didn't jump on immediately and ride out of her shop, but instead guided the bike while walking next to it, as though I were chatting to a shy pony. Only when I was away from any watchful eyes did I swing my leg over, let my feet scrabble to find the pedals and move forward, inch by wobbly inch.

The stony bike paths were beautiful. They could take me to river edges, where poplar fluff of summer drifted like fairy crowns caught in the water's lip. Across paddocks, glossy mares with manes of spun gold tossed and snuffled in their fields. Surrounded by such beauty, how could I not be able to ride? *How could such things not be possible?*

I managed to go straight for a little while, but then I got the wobbles and couldn't master the art of turning without ending in a jack-knife position. Which at one point, threatened to topple me into the river, a three-metre drop below. I returned the bike to the German lady before part of it embedded into me permanently.

I spent most of my childhood balancing on a gymnastic beam. I found it easier doing a handstand on ten centimetres than I did pedalling on a road ten metres wide. During my attempts to learn to ride my mum ran after me, holding onto the bike, steadying me on countless occasions. 'I've got you, I've got you!' she shouted before letting go.

For a few seconds, I held it. I was riding! My white wicker basket leading the way. Pink painted flower handles glinting. Two wheels spinning madly in the dirt. It happened in an instant – I tilted awkwardly – lost momentum – and came smacking down cheek and elbow first, hitting the earth. When my head stopped spinning and the world around me settled, I wheeled that contraption into the back of our dusty garage and left here there, to rust.

At our Kenyan campsite, we are waiting for a new bus, a new driver. Sarah also offers an escape route: at dusk a bus will arrive at camp to take those who want to leave back to Nairobi, to the airport.

We could all so easily go home.

Until then, we have hours to fill, so when a local guide arrives offering a trip through the national park – a twenty-six kilometre ride by bike – I say yes. *How hard can it be,* I think, *to ride a bike?*

**THE WOODEN** gates to the Masai Mara are as tall as a two-storey building. Cracked and peeling green paint. Summer sun bleaches the sky, so it's dazzling and white. On either side of the gate, green hills and sandy pathways. Far off in the distance, the earth erupts in a series of rocks and boulders, crouching on top of each other, tall as a monolith, their pointed fingers reaching into the sky, trying to pierce the clouds.

The tour is led by a young, local man with wiry thin arms and wide eyes. He's wearing jeans that sit right below the slash of his bottom, revealing white boxer shorts that read KLEINE around the band. He has short, curly hair and reflective Oakleys perched on top. Around his neck he wears a knotted red bandana.

He introduces himself as Kobi. We follow him through the gates stepping over: dust, paint, old shoes, rubber casings, a small slender white rock that could once have been a pinky finger. Off to the left, a small dusty shack sits, a mottled green. Inside old bikes, sans helmets, are lined and waiting. He walks towards the smallest blue bike, a rusty old thing, leaning against an old splintering fence and wheels it towards me while it shrieks like something alive. I feel quite similarly – about shrieking – and think perhaps this makes us a good pair. The blue bike is as rusty and filthy as the pink one I left in a garage twenty years ago would be now.

Shamil hops on a tall black bike with ease, one leg over, and starts riding away. He yells something over his shoulder about giraffes, but the rest of his words are swallowed by the wind. He stands on his pedals with grace, looking like a jockey heading down the straight. Ailie whoops into the air like a kid on Christmas morning, mounting her white bike like a gallant steed and pedals furiously to catch up with Shamil.

Ant looks at me, 'You got this, possum?'

'In the bag,' I tell her. She pedals away on a slender red bike. Like a woman from the 1920s, she could only have been more graceful had she chosen to ride side saddle.

I start off a little wobbly. Okay, a lot. A dust cloud billows in front of me and I stop to cough and clear my nose. Each time I hop back on I hope it will be easy. Everyone else makes it look easy. Despite panting and puffing, it takes all my might to get my bike to go forward.

I look ahead at the large rocky hills. A dust cloud puffs. I sneeze. I can't see anything. My tyre hits a rock. Suddenly I'm skidding in the gravel. When the dust settles, it appears I have managed to do a 180-degree turn and am facing the entrance. Is this a sign?

I can still back out. The exit is only a hundred metres away. I could say thanks, hand over blue rusty and bid adieu to Kobi. Back at camp, I can lie by the river somewhere and watch hippos and drink Coke out of glass bottles. I could swat away mosquitos, make a creamy coffee, eat buttery toast until I am stuffed, and finish reading the rest of my book.

Kobi stops and looks back at me. 'You okay?'

'I'm not sure I can ride a bike,' my voice wavers.

He looks at me like I've just told him I don't know how to *breathe*.

I pick up the bike like a frustrated toddler and stamp it down with force. THE. RIGHT. WAY. When it happens a second time just minutes later, I feel like screaming. It isn't until I see the sign hanging in white above the entrance that I understand. *Hell's Gates.*

It seems I've followed my own Virgil in the form of Kobi willingly into Hell. And here we are waiting. I'm thinking of everything – the truck accident, the unmarked speed bumps, riding a bike when I can't. *What if I die? What if I hurt myself? What if I fall? What if I fail?*

But also: *What if it's magnificent? What if I'm happier? What if this place changes me?*

These are the questions people asked me, before I left. Ahead the grey clouds fill the Kenyan sky. A few stripes of sun still find the ground. The land spreads out before me, honey-coloured sand, soft-grey rock sides. I blink and the sun beams, then, the muted swish of zebra tails flicking flies off rumps. The wind comes fast. Sand gets in my mouth, on my face. My eyes start to water. I think of Dante, standing amongst the rotting souls of the underworld, fearful but pressing on.

'Let go,' is all Kobi says.

I think he meant, *Let's go*, but then his words swim in my head. I realise they are by a strike of fate much better placed for this moment.

My feet find the pedals. I push and heave – it isn't easy – and begin to move. My knees creak like the bike, my bottom hurts from the hard seat. My thighs feel hot and thick and out of practice. My breath sounds like the short, wheezy heaves of someone with asthma. I sweat and grunt and my face becomes quickly caked in a layer of dust.

I think of people at home and work – sitting at desks, going to meetings, sweating on buses, cramped on the train, stuck in traffic. It makes me pedal faster.

Eventually, I catch up with the others. When we ride as far as we can go on bikes, we leave them perched against each other and begin to climb the rock faces, metres high, without rope. Has the gorilla trek helped? I find myself discovering muscles I don't know I have, pulling me up, helping me find balance in tiny footholds.

Sweat drips into our eyes. At small ledges we stop to catch our breath, downing water thirstily, before continuing upwards, grabbing plants and rock edges, working our way towards the sky.

We find respite for a few minutes at one of the highest points, a peak that overlooks the entire park. We are as high, if not higher, than the birds. We can't hear anything below. Instead of the wind reverberating from the cavernous mouths of caves, it's utterly silent. The earth unfolds before us. Lizards creep across the sand near our feet, tiny feet, quick heads dart to and fro, hearing things we don't. The sun has grown in size and rips a hole through the clouds; the weight of it softens us – I feel like dozing. The colours of the earth seep together – mottled olive and spongy ochre. Someone drops a hair band and it disappears. The world drops away into tiers of rock, sloping and falling. We stand then, the five of us, too close to the edge. Despite the possibility of falling, we think instead of flying.

Before the sun sets we descend through the layers of rock, back out the way we came, and begin the long pedal back to the gates. I can't feel my bottom for the constant bumping of bike over rock sending shock waves into my legs. Ant is behind me and calls out something, but I have momentum now and don't turn around.

Sometimes when we look back we lose the momentum to keep going forward, finding the places where we were, rather than those we should be.

I keep facing forward, feeling glorious.

When we return our bikes to Kobi, the Gates of Hell close behind us. I look over at Ant and say, 'Yes.'

'Yes?' she asks.

'Yes. We keep going.'

And I keep repeating Dante's words to myself like a mantra:

> *Do not be afraid; our fate*
> *Cannot be taken from us; it is a gift.*

**THE COUNTRY** is parched. We're told it's normal for it to be so hot, but even moving feels unforgiving. It takes every ounce of energy just to lift our legs.

Closing my eyes, I wait for the wind. It doesn't arrive. Thirst marks every second. We drink more than we ever have. We pass a cow lying by the side of the road, her belly distended, her thick lips parted. Her gasp for air haunts me even now, the spittle bubbling and frothing like a toad as she grunts, but is unable to get up. Too hot. Too old. Too late. I want to stay with her, to reach down, to pat her shin, to take her large head in my lap and let her pass like that, with someone hanging onto her, but the game park driver steps on the accelerator and we keep going. The sand burns in the sun, hot and hard. The wind picks up the dry ground and tosses it aloft. It finds its way into every crevice. There is sand in our truck, on our seats, in our hair, crunching in our teeth. Ragged red tree trunks are exposed like blood and flesh. The skin has split and the bark hangs off in strips like a long laceration.

Everywhere feels dry. I can't remember how it felt to be cold and blue in Uganda, when the water in my body had frozen, icicles forming on the rungs of my ribs, splintering my chest. We haven't seen water in days, and I am beginning to dry out. I have started – like a selkie – to gaze out at the horizon longing to catch a glimpse of water.

## ways to come home

My hands are stained with the dirt of this land. It won't budge under water or time. My eyebrows grow thicker and more quickly than I remember, and I discard my tweezers one day into a passing town's bin because, *who cares?* I stop applying make-up in the mornings, even tinted moisturiser, and move through the day, my face nude.

At first this scares me. It has been years since I discovered that my face was growing its own dark brown shade of distaste. In patches, my skin has been consistently darkening. As I went from doctor to expert to dermatologist, they mentioned words like *hyperpigmentation* and *melasma*. Each of them wrote hurried prescriptions for creams and salves and ointments that made my wallet lighter, but never my skin.

I allowed bold beauticians to zap it with lasers and peel layers off with chemicals. Once, I took home a face of puffed, new red raw skin and had to stay indoors, and out of sunlight for a week. And still the dark patches remained. Some had become thicker, darker, until almost black. Worst I think was the spread of it underneath my nose, and on my upper lip. From far away it was as though I'd taken a finger of dirt and wiped a clean line, or more unfortunately, a moustache. I wonder if perhaps these marks are oozing from the past, through gaps I have allowed, parts of myself desperately trying to come out.

I look at myself in cracked mirrors of old bathrooms and see myself as these brown spots walking around. I do not see my red lips or my hazel eyes or my long tangle of brown hair, any of which could possibly be beautiful.

Fellow travellers have also begun a stripping-back process. They discard hair gel and moisturiser and coconut body butters and things that mattered to us at home. Our hair is left to how nature intended it. No straighteners or dryers, mine hangs heavy, wavy and thick down my back.

Our legs scaly for a few days, perhaps a week, have begun to remember how to make their own moisture. Body balms are no longer needed.

We speed along highways further south, away from the central dry sauna of Tanzania and edge closer to the capital, Dar Es Salaam, sitting squat on the coast. I am grateful for the humidity that begins to collect in the wind. As the air gathers more moisture, it makes us swelter and sweat. Until we all smell like day old ham hanging from the eaves.

**THE BELL** in the stone tower tolls two. Loud chimes strike off the sandstone walls, reverberating around the town square. A flock of seagulls take flight, coasting on the onshore breeze, riding higher into the coral blue sky. The waves whip froth and the breeze carries specks of water landing on our shoulders. The ferry docks in pure aquamarine water. Transparent to the bottom, I can make out schools of fish darting in and out of the wooden pylons. The sea stretches in all directions like a lazy cat.

Stone Town, the main port of Zanzibar, is welcoming. I feel like I'm in Europe rather than Africa. Arched tunnels. Sandstone buildings. Grand buildings. Palaces. Winding staircases. Bougainvillea-lined streets. Cafes with roughly written chalkboards, specials – crepes, seafood, ice cream. Ice cream! It's been so long since we had ice cream.

Bicycles zoom past. People saunter slowly, stop to talk to old friends, taking time to light a cigarette and blow smoke into the cloudless sky. Green grass perfectly cut, signs that say *do not step here*. But we do anyway because it's softer than plush carpet and our feet have only felt dust and sand and rock for weeks. An old wall crumbles near us. Ruins from history, when Zanzibar used to be a trading spice market and the origins of the first black slave market. We've been returned to a lost time.

The first thing we do is order an iced coffee. 'Yes, double ice cream. Yes please. You have wi-fi?' Oh, I think I'm in love.

As Ant and I take a walk down to the water's edge, she picks a bright fuchsia bougainvillea and sticks it behind her ear. The water, crystal clear; the sand so white in the sun's brilliant reflection that we need sunglasses. We hike up our skirts and dip our toes in. Warm. Who would have thought Africa had such a tropical hideaway?

Stony streets – where will they take us? Jewellery shops hidden down alleyways so narrow, we walk shoulder to shoulder and still touch the walls. Parasols for sale. Hematite rings. Handwoven silk scarves. Stuffed with ice cream, we keep walking. Discovering. Through a window we see a woman bent over the sink scrubbing at potatoes. Guards stand and smoke outside a stone facade turret. We walk the streets for hours, only returning to the hotel after the sun loses her hold and slips into the sea.

I dream that night of the delectable lightness that comes with being near the ocean – and wake up feeling new.

**ON A** Tuesday morning we leave Stone Town and drive across the island in old minivans heading east. Plantations are abundant. Dates and bananas, palm trees reach into the sky large like giant beanstalks. They're tall enough to graze the clouds.

The island feels distinctly Fijian in the east. Long white sandy beaches. Palm trees and coconuts. Hibiscus flowers, wild red and sunshine yellow. Frangipanis, white and muted yellow, soft pink, falling around us. Bursts of colour everywhere.

We stay in simple beach-side huts. Cool tile floors. Thatched roofs. White walls. A rough timber shelf for our clothes. Before we unpack, Ant and I run barefoot to the beach. I need a swim more than ever. We leave a string of clothes as we disrobe running towards the water's edge.

Dive into the coolness, there aren't any waves. I swim out, and out, further and further until the beach starts to disappear. I dive and duck. Feel the gentle glide of the current. Float on my back. Watch the clouds drift past. Water in my ears. I can't hear anything but the beat of my own heart.

Underneath is another world. Fish bigger than my hand, and quick, they avoid my legs treading water, darting like black bullets. Resting on the sandy floor are sea urchins, black with spindle spikes, each tip carrying soft poison enough to numb a hand for days.

Crystal clear water as far as I can see. Old dhows, African fishing boats, sail by, coming in with their catch of the day, fish flapping on the old wooden decks, their torn sails flapping in the sea breeze. I could float here forever.

I can't keep away from the water. Every time I'm dry I dive back in again. My skin tans quickly. I turn the deep black of a kalamata olive.

The beach sunbeds are made from timber frames and twine crisscrossed into rectangular patterns. It may as well be wire, biting into our skin leaving red raw marks. We have to turn ourselves like pigs on a spit every three minutes or it starts to draw blood.

Before dusk I drag myself away from the ocean. We arrive back at the hut dazed by sun and happiness. Time to unpack. Ant and I turn our backpacks upside down, take out every single item of clothing, pack and refold it onto shelves. We even HANG them.

The bed, a massive king size, has starchy white cotton sheets. We could lay spread-eagled like starfish and still not find each other. The honey-coloured tiles cool our feet after the burning sand. The windows are shuttered and we can choose whether to let the daylight in or not. We leave the door open and gusts of salty sea air sigh into our room. The housekeeper leaves a lone, yellow flower in a sky-blue vase. It catches the last fragments of day and shines as bright as a sun.

Ant makes me a coffee from the instant sludge and I recline on the king-size bed, treasuring each sip. I can stretch my weary body across the white sheets and sleep. I close my eyes and try to imagine what life would be like if we stay here. How brown we'd be! How relaxed. Would we become sailors? Or fisherwomen? Or would we set up a transient tourist stall offering massages? Yes, that did seem much more like us. Would we get bored? Would we be lured in time, back to the mainland?

Ant unpacks and retires to the bathroom to prepare, as she calls it. She leaves the door open and I, stiff from salt and sea spray walk in without knocking, to wash my face. She is somewhat awkwardly mounted on the side of the bath tweezing her bikini line. I am astonished to discover she plucks each hair individually.

'Do you have some abnormal tolerance to pain?' Long gone is the covering up of our parts. Her sitting near the toilet plucking at her nether region doesn't faze either of us.

She shrugs. 'I just know it has to be done.'

When she has finished, we take turns to shower and slip into floaty summer dresses. Dinner is forgotten. Instead the Americans, Scott and Steve, mix flat, warm cola with cheap vodka and cheaper bourbon.

Down the beach, a club is playing old music from the eighties. We dance outside on the cool sand, the wind flapping our dresses and skirts, our arms waving to the full moon under a clear sky. Travellers and tourists, hipsters and hippies, Africans and westerners, tonight it doesn't matter who you are, we all dance together. Hugging like friends who've loved each other for years.

Cheap African bourbon can have that effect.

**SARAH WARNS** us the ferry journey between the Tanzanian mainland and Zanzibar can be rough. The way she says it I think we should be preparing for imminent death. Before we leave she opens a small black bag, revealing an apothecary of pills. She points to each capsule – nausea, sea sickness, stomach cramps, headaches, migraines. There are patches, herbal drops and mints. Five packets of breath mints. 'You'll need them,' she nods.

So I am pleasantly relieved when our trip to Zanzibar is as smooth as gliding across glass. We sit at the bow of the boat, our legs tucked under the metal rungs. Skimming small waves with ease, we watch as the sunlight dashes across the surface of the water beside us. Sea birds and gulls crow close to the ship's starboard side and easily ride the streams of wind wake.

Whizzing across the sea, the land disappears and then, without an anchor point, we have no indication of how fast we are really going. I get a sense we are nowhere, and instead of frightening me, it thrills me. I love lying back on the white deck and watching a sailor's blue sky, feeling the sun soak into every joint. Heat makes us drowsy and there are moments when I catch myself in that limbo state between being awake and nodding off. The ferry has rocked us all into contentment. Going back, we assume, would be the same.

Going back, Sarah leaves a day before us to organise campsites and groceries back in Dar Es Salaam.

'I need someone to lead the group while I'm away,' she tells us. 'They'll just look after the passports, get everyone on the ferry, and off safely at the other side.'

But Sarah had either been indulging in cheap bourbon or had a moment of sheer delusion, because she picked me.

In the morning we fill up on our last delights of Zanzibar – tiny pastries that come in boxes and are tied with string. Are we really backpackers? Fresh orange juice from chilled terracotta carafes poured by gracious waitresses as we sit in the open garden of our hotel. Someone's curtain has been sucked out their ground floor window and it billows and flutters in the breeze. I could easily be in Morocco, the intricate mosaic tiles, deep colours of ruby, emerald and sapphire delicately twisted upon white glazed tiles – we could be many places.

We stop, just one last time, at the cafe we found without looking on our first day. The one just by that pebbled bridge, near where the harbour water stains the pavement at high tide, past the man on a bicycle selling fish from tubs stacked with ice. Here we have ice coffee, again, with a frosted shot glass of toffee ice cream.

The rest of the town has woken while we have idled away time sipping lattes. The sun has tipped herself in-between buildings, warming the stone. Stepping out of the cafe, the town buzzes with life. Ant and I take the time, just a few minutes, to go back to the jewellery man who has a shopfront decorated in silks. There are cerulean scarves, and ruby walls. The sun catches coloured glass Moroccan lanterns, casting a mystical kaleidoscope on the farthest yellow wall. There are wonderful bronzed elephant heads (wall pieces), and small flecked gold fish that are not only beautifully designed, but hold your keys together too.

'Morning,' the owner greets us from behind a small makeshift desk, sitting in an upholstered red chair, sipping his morning coffee.

We step into the perfectly cool and shaded shop and inside it smells like rose tea and incense – a stick of it is burning on the floor, the carpet catching the ashings. Ant picks out a hematite ring, a slender band that hugs her right ring finger. She wants to stay and feel the silk scarves.

'There could be something in here I desperately need,' she tells me. 'Do we have time for ice cream?'

'No, we don't,' I say as the temporary tour guide, I must think sensibly.

We turn away from the town where life whizzes past. I lead Ant to the prearranged meeting point and from there, herd the group to the pier. I gather their passports in a large stack. We're stamped out of Zanzibar (even though we're still in Tanzania), at their immigration office – a small un-air conditioned wooden shack riddled with flies.

Onboard the ferry, Zanzibar's elegant coastline looks as if it has been dreamt – dotted tropical palms, magnificent bell towers and curved stone buildings radiant in the midday sun. Conditions in the harbour are idyllic, with the sun high in the sky.

We sit at the bow, each of us, Ailie, Tiff, Ant and myself, tucking our legs underneath the bottom metal rung, our chins resting on the top one. Sea salt cools our arms and stings our lips, forming a crust that has to be licked every few minutes. Chugging slowly away from the port, we leave a diesel streak hanging in the air. The boat sings its last horn, a deep whale sound, as we find open seas.

**THE OCEAN** current rushes in. Ripples. A small swell. Waves hit the hull of the boat like tiny high-fives. Another set emerges several minutes later, growing in size; the height of a small desk, no thicker than a pane of glass. Lavender – thin enough light can pass through.

The captain changes course, pointing the bow to the left. We lean away from the waves; the boat creaks portside. Rolls slightly. Rights herself. As she does, the water pulls back, sucks away; we can almost see the rocks below, the lengths to the bottom of the ocean. It's a cavern. A rounded vacuum. The ferry is suddenly rocked nose-first into it. We tilt forward. Thump once. Skid upward on the crest of the next wave. My heart quickens a beat as another wave rushes towards us, thumping into the hull, propelling us into the air. We land heavily. *Ouch.* We grimace and grab our bottoms.

Ten minutes later, the large waves become tidal ones. Sea giants. Large looming walls of navy water. Tinged with green, and that makes them seem mad. They thump us from every angle. We are tossed into the air, hovering for seconds, long seconds, airborne before crashing to the bow edge. Up again. We smack our legs into each other. Tiff lands on my lap, we start to laugh, but no sooner do we realise than we are tossed again.

In the trough of the waves, the ferry rocks dangerously low to the right side. Ant, her hair wet and plastered to her face, looks giddy with joy. Ailie yells crazily into the wind like she's Lieutenant Dan from *Forest Gump*.

My stomach knots. I feel the foul burn of caffeine up my oesophagus wanting to exit the way it came in. A massive wave cracks so loud over the bow the boat may split in half.

'I don't like this,' I say.

The seascape is frothing and tormented. For several minutes we are battered by waves. Up ahead, a monstrous wave looms. The closer it comes, the more weight, the more water it gathers. So thick and inky navy, it begins to blot out the sun. It has to be at least a storey tall, large enough to tip the ferry, large enough to roll us all into the sea.

'Hold on!' someone yells.

I reach for the railing, but my saturated hands lose grip. When the wave starts curling on top of us I say, 'Oh God,' and wonder if it is the start of a prayer or a eulogy.

I close my eyes. It hits us quickly and with such force, I go flying across the deck. Rather, I imagine how it feels to be knocked in the head by a block of concrete. My cheeks are stung red-raw. The boat lurches wildly. Not anchored by anything, I slide sharply back towards the bow. With full force my back smacks into a steel pole – the only thing keeping me from falling off.

Before I can stand up, a crescendo of waves hit the hull. I'm smacked against the steel rung twice. Both of the waves recede together, forming a trough at the same time. A lull. A breather.

I seize the opportunity. Standing up, turning my back to the waves. Facing the open, wet, slippery puddle of the bow. There is safety at each end – the rung where I stand now at the point, and the door at least five metres away. But in the middle, is no-mans land, a place you mustn't find yourself when the wave hits. If the ferry lurches to the side, there is nothing to grab. Anyone could slide, so easily, right off the edge.

*Go. Go.* I walk fast but carefully, like a child on ice, quick little flurry steps – careful not to slip. With my back to the bow, I don't see the wave coming. It must be huge. Someone shouts. When it crashes, the furl of its fury foam reaches my head. The boat sinks into the trough of the wave's wake so violently it knocks me to my knees. I hit hard against the deck's steel surface.

'Help!' I scream, spotting a man gripping onto the metal door. 'Get me inside!'

He reaches as far as he can stretch. I take an actual leap of faith – I can slide off the end so easily if the boat rocks even slightly. He heaves open the heavy casing, stumbles through, and pulls me with him just before another wave cracks like a whip against the bow. The door slams behind us.

Inside, people are screaming and crying and retching. The entire galley stinks of vomit. The boat rocks violently to the right, and on such an angle, trails of vomit run down the aisle, between the seats, on the seats, down the back of seats. Carrot dinner. This morning's eggy breakfast. Regurgitated. Chunky.

Women are moaning, and children are passed out in the aisle, crumpled bodies. Bile snakes under the seats towards limp fainted faces as the boat lurches again.

People look miserable, grey and ill. An old woman hunches over and throws up into a bag. The smell and sound of fresh gagged spew is too much. Her husband reaches for a bag and just makes it before the vomit explodes from his mouth.

I run down the aisle, leaping like a wild woman over trails and puddles as best as I can. *Why am I so ill-planned for this trip and wearing open-toed flip flops?* I try not to show how horrified I am as I reach the door marked exit, only for it not to open. It's locked. It won't budge.

'Open it. Open please,' I mouth to the man outside. He looks at me and turns away.

The boat is now rocking so violently that I am having trouble standing. It dips low to the left, so low the side windows are submerged in water. A door on the farthest port side unhinges and flings open.

I consider breaking through the small window no larger than my head at the top of the door and pulling myself out. On the other side of the boat is a similar exit door. When the boat levels for a split second, I leap over a woman clutching her stomach in the middle of the centre aisle, and a boy dribbling milky vomit trails into a bin. I grab onto the door handle, yank it wide open and step outside. Sea air.

Outside too, the decks are crowded with women and men and children, all heaving. The telltale acid burps pre-vomitus, start with one man, then echo across the crowd, like they are catching. Soon everyone is making gagging sounds.

Slinking between seasick figures, I am careful not to step on toes and hands, whispering 'sorry' when I do, and then realising these people don't even notice. Everyone's passed out.

There is an empty spot at the very back left corner of the boat. I gratefully step into the space and lean against the back of the boat. My legs wobble, give way. I slide into a crouch.

A wave hits the starboard side and the gate I am holding onto nearly unhinges and unlocks. The metal makes a whining sound and I envision the gate opening, and me being flung into the sea without anyone noticing.

A woman vomits into a bag and lets it go into the breeze. It whips a metre into the wind, hovers there for a second before the strong undercurrents whip the bag back towards the boat. It lands slightly open – she hasn't tied it – on my face. A stranger's vomit runs down my cheek. Part of it trickles down my lip and almost into my mouth. A wave slaps overboard, rinsing the rest into my clothes and hair. I taste engine diesel. It burns my mouth.

In the distance, I see land. So far away I can't make people out on the shore. I can barely distinguish the different shapes and colours – olive and honey – between the distant hills and the cottages perched upon them. *Oh, thank you,* I think. *Let's go home.*

But instead of hugging the coastline, or turning towards it, we stay out in the ocean. If the boat suddenly unshackled herself and started sinking, I couldn't swim the distance. It's at least a mile, possibly five. This continues another hour.

When we dock in the late afternoon I am drenched and exhausted. I take five shaky steps down the plank and step onto the dirt. I slide to my hands and knees, dripping, and try to kiss the ground. But I end up collapsing into it, battering myself in dirt, like a fish ready for frying.

I make a loud declaration to the sky, to no-one in particular.

'Next time I'm flying.'

**LAKE MALAWI** is extraordinarily big. I say this like I've encountered a massive bus, or the world's largest ocean liner. But both could fit on this lake several times over and there would still be plenty of room. In fact, you could lift up the entire country of Ireland and toss it in the lake and it would be submerged on all sides.

I leave the unpacking (this place doesn't have hangers), for later. This lake is like a beach. There is sand, yellow and burning hot in the sun. Volleyball nets. Deckchairs face the lake and cricket bats and tennis balls are ready for a beach game. And waves. Pounding, crashing, breaking waves. Further out in the lake are spots to scuba dive, fish that are rare, unseen in other parts of the world. A jumping rock for those that like the adrenaline buzz.

The advice I was given by Australian doctors plainly is this: do not swim in Lake Malawi. It is apparently teeming with the dreaded *Bilharzia*, a parasitic worm that's carried in certain types of sea snail. These worms kindly enter by burrowing into your skin before settling down in the blood vessels surrounding the bladder or large intestine. Here they enjoy themselves, producing millions of eggs living happily for up to twenty years causing the host all sorts of ill side effects (fever, fatigue, liver and spleen enlargement, and, in some rare cases, cancer of the bladder).

A friend who travelled to Africa some years ago on a similar route shared this story days before I left for Kenya. A man on her trip experienced a strange bite on his leg that he remembered occurring somewhere along the coastal region of Malawi. Within a few days it had grown substantially, going from the size of a small pimple to a boil. A week later my friend, also a nurse, took a closer look.

Inside the stretched skin, taut and white, she could see the throbbing pulse of larvae. A tsetse fly had laid her eggs, millions of them, in the nook of his upper thigh and he was hosting them for birth. With rum poured in his mouth and the bottle emptied over his leg, she cut his thigh open with a scalpel. He roared with pain. The gash opened was deep and straight, an inch long. Immediately pupae fell out, writhing and scattering, looking for a new place to live. The entire camp, shoes at the ready, stepped and squashed every last one into the ground.

Should stories like this stop me?

They don't. I dive in.

The strange absence of sea unnerves me. No salt. No sting. It tastes like tap water. As if I'm swimming in an enormous, warm bath.

Ant and I duck underwater, holding our breath. Unlike Zanzibar, we can't see the bottom. We can hardly see in front of us, the rich royal navy water hiding everything from sight. Sometimes when I open my eyes for a second underwater, before quickly closing them again, it looks like a midnight sky, the tiny dots of sunlight that make it this far down glinting like stars.

Some swim half the lake, to the jumping rock in the middle, propelling themselves off a ten-metre cliff plunging into the inky depths below. Others strap oxygen tanks to their backs, Ailie and Tiff find cichlid fish – the maternal mouth breeder – well known for spitting out and then swallowing back her young.

Later, we paddle far from the shore and watch the people sunbaking become distant dots and blurs. The dazzling, cobalt sky is without a cloud. This lake water has streams and tides, and at times we feel the tug of it, pulling us further away from the shore. Grateful that if we did indeed ride a current, we'd only ride it to the opposite shore.

The lake is busy every hour of the day. It offers a place to bathe, to swim, to wash, to work, to gather at night and cook on small pot fires, to eat, and to drink. During the day the friendly locals gather to wash and beat their clothes against the rocks. For a small price, they do ours too.

Groups of women, some with babies, arrive with more freshly tied stacks of clothes. Mountains of our clothes once stained brown – so dark we thought they would never be clean – are now white again. They are miracle workers.

My washing returns stiff and starched, folded neatly, pants perfectly creased, shirts with collars stiff and starchy, piled on top of each other in a pyramid of sizes; smallest at the top, tied with a piece of string, flourished with a twine bow. I inhale the freshness; the kind that doesn't come from laundry powder or liquid, but from nature, rinsed in lake water, dried under the sun, pressed between rocks.

'Could you hold him?' I look up to see a mother asking me to hold her baby while she unloads her washing.

At first I am reluctant. *A baby? Strapped to my back? He looks happy exactly where he is.*

'Go on,' she smiles, and pushes my arm.

'Yes,' I say, 'Okay then.'

He is swaddled and tied to my back. A sarong is carefully wrapped around him and then knotted at my stomach and neck. At first I'm afraid I'll drop him as I walk around, and hold my right hand to support his bottom. I'm not sure the cloth is strong enough, the knots tight enough, to stop him from falling right through.

'Let it go,' a woman waves. 'Yes, relax,' another lady says.

Slowly I ease my arm away. The baby remains perfectly in place, chewing on the edge of the cloth like cud. I watch him over my left shoulder, expecting him to cry, pinned as he is against the milky skin of a stranger, but he doesn't.

He accompanies me to the truck, back to my tent and around the bus once, then twice. As we near the gate we both explore the smell of the pyrantheum flower that grows in thick clumps to one side of the camp. All along he chews the edge of the cloth. Sometimes I catch him staring at me as I stare at him, both of us seeming slightly surprised to find the other one still there.

When he is finally unstrapped from my back, the women retreat towards the lake – new clothes are waiting to be washed and pressed. I wave until they are out of sight. As they turn the corner, does he turn his head? Or do I imagine it?

'You'd make a good mother,' Ant says later as we're cutting carrots for dinner.

'Would I?' I say, surprised.

She starts peeling garlic, removing their paper-thin casings.

'Yes,' she nods. 'There is something about you.'

She looks over, and I feel her eyes studying me. 'I just get that feeling.'

A gust of gnats swarm past our faces. It's a windy evening, almost jacket weather. I look at the leaves fluttering in the breeze. Mumble something about it getting cold. Stroll over to the tent and pick around for my cardigan. Inside my heart beats like a Roman drum.

Her comment is not without irony, for I have been a mother.

And I have had two.

**LOCAL MALAWIAN** men eagerly wait for us outside the gates of our campsite. Clapping. Shouting. Herding us.

'You want to snorkel? Jewellery box? Wall hanging? Key ring? Marry ju wana?'

'I do want a jewellery box, actually,' I tell the young guy who introduces himself as Raffa. 'With a starfish. Some brilliant stars. Like a night sky in Africa. Ocean waves.'

He frowns. 'You mean all together, the stars in the waves?'

I laugh. 'No, no.'

Raffa gives me a piece of paper and asks me to draw it.

I lean down over the paper catching the smell of his sweat without deodorant, the ripe earthiness of musk. I sketch badly, an outline of waves, and it looks more like a wobbly Sydney Opera House. I write above it in capital letters WAVES. (Yes, my drawing skills are so poor that I have to name it.) I sketch a wonky starfish and label it too.

'Do you get what I mean? I'm sure you can do much better,' and hand over my stick-figure drawings.

My star is so lopsided it appears half of it has already been sucked into a black hole.

'And you pay for this fifty dollars!' Raffa grins, beginning the bargaining dance Malawians love.

We laugh. I barter him down to twelve dollars and a pair of my old white sandals. Who wants my cruddy sandals anyway?

Ant and I wander around the tent of their talent. Elephant masks. Little stools, gorillas carved into the legs. Jewellery boxes of all shapes, pre-made and lacquered in a honey-brown glaze. Key rings, shapes of Africa each once precise and wonderful, whittled in and out, each inlet, with such care. And selling for less than a carton of milk.

In the corner, specialty items left to dry in the sun after a coat or two of varnish, carved specifically for individuals who have selected the animals, the shapes, the colours, the size – chairs, boxes, chests that open on giant hinges and squeak perfectly as though they are antique. They will be boxed up, padded and swaddled, shuffled onto boats or planes and couriered back home where they will sit in the corner of houses, proudly on display.

Ant has selected as much as she can hold – ebony necklaces and glossed black figurines of hippos and leopards.

'I want that too!' she exclaims, picking up a high-backed chair.

These men are true artists. Along each caramel leg has been carved the animals Africa is known for – hippo, lion, elephant and leopard. At the top across the back of the chair, facing outwards, two cheetah eyes on alert.

'Yes, and how will you go transporting a wooden chair in your backpack?' I ask.

Reluctantly, she returns the piece to the corner where it sits elegantly awaiting another buyer. She settles instead for a small globe of the world, wooden and carved. Dipped in wax, it comes apart in half so you can study both the northern and southern hemispheres, holding each in your palm. Inside is a perfect place for rings, or notes from friends, or just the rocks and stones and tumbled lake glass we find each day we saunter along the shore, in shapes we never thought possible.

Forty minutes under the tent, without a breeze, and it feels we have all started to breathe each other's exhales. Stuffy and smelly. I've had enough of shopping. Thankfully, Ant has too.

We wave goodbye to Raffa at the end of the driveway, where stone gives way to parched earth. Then with quick feet we run over burning sand, down to the lake.

**EVERYONE FEELS** like we're on a holiday from our holiday. There is a certain zest in the air. All day the beach weather holds. Unblinkable blue skies. Sun scorched sands. By late morning it burns the soles of our feet. People hop and curse and jump into patches of damp sand or shade when they can, balancing on one foot, sometimes on tiptoes.

When the heat falls like fire at midday, everyone retreats in haste. Even the water burns like a boiling bath. We lay on beds in stuffy rooms and let the fans spin at top speed sending dust and fly carcasses across the room, some landing on our bare legs.

The sunlight, like hands, reaches in, finds its way into our hut and glares at us, bouncing off every surface – the mirror, the windows, the fridge door.

Lunch is ready. A smorgasbord of fish and salads and bread rolls, finally edible. Soft and squishy, with a slight crunch to the skin. Exactly as you wish white bread to be. Are there bakers here?

We take our portable fold-out seats to the hut by the lake, where we watch the water, shaded, as intently as if watching the football finals. Waves crash onto the sand. How can this be a lake?

Bees and flies and mosquitos duck around our heads and we shoo them from our food. A lizard runs between our feet. Ants traverse my toes like a mountain, a steady string of them marching over my big toe. I don't care to flick them off, but stay watching them instead.

We swim for hours. Our fingers prune. Our toes shrivel. My skin becomes waterlogged white. The sun finds its way to the bottom of the lake, and we sit under the water, watching the sky from below. The water turns a peregrine blue. Everything is filled with light, capturing it, reflecting it straight back up to the surface.

We stay in the lake until the sun forgives the land and dims her intensity. She leaves the sky that night with an indigo blush that lasts longer than other dusky evenings. The night flowers open and everywhere smells like honey-sap.

I feel tired but don't want to sleep. In the last streams of light, everyone heads to the bar for beer. I emerge reluctantly from the water and choose a last spot of sun to dry off. I can hear the sound of tipsy people from the bar, but am much happier walking along the water's edge, watching the evening sky turn lavender, pumpkin and then a royal navy. I stroll ankle deep in the inky water for hundreds of metres. Listening to the soft rush of the tide wash up and down the sand.

By then the sky is deep velvet, encrusted with stars. Their light catches the lips of the waves and they filter through the water, like diamond filaments scattered and glinting. I stand in the whitewash letting the fresh water run sweet and cool over my feet.

As the night deepens, I find myself feeling more awake than tired. I'm always energised by the water. Soothed. Calmed. Grounded. Is it strange that something that constantly moves is the same thing that makes me feel so still?

I realise when I was in Sydney, in an office, in my car, even in a restaurant or cafe, I was surrounded by walls. Perhaps they used to make me feel safe, but now I can see how they stifle.

In Africa, we have dinner under the stars. Lunch by the lake. Breakfast as the sun slips from behind night's hood. Toast with a soft-boiled egg. Cups of heavenly coffee, thick and dark. The cool cement of the floor, scrubbed cement with a thin lick of green paint. I brush my feet over it, grains of sand try their best to exfoliate my heels.

In fact, we do most things outdoors, and even at night, when we don't want to sleep inside, sometimes we pull out the small thin slip of mattress and lay underneath the moon, the stars as our roof.

Being outside in Africa, you gain a certain sense of cycles. Of time. It's hard to miss the light, the seasons, the turn of both when you are standing, a wondrous spectator, in it. And it's particularly nice to let anything and anyone come and go as they please.

I walk back to our wooden cabin, its rough edges, wonky shape, a silhouette jutting into the sky. Down below on the beach the waves continue to roll, a pleasant symmetry of sound, marking the breath of water – in and out, in and out. Shallow. Deep. Shallow. Deep.

The scent of Africa is familiar now, like home – cedar and milkwood, and the fragrance of smoke from beach bonfires that have licked the night sky.

**AT THE** top of our long, dusty driveway is a small Malawian school. Four demountable classrooms huddle in a semicircle. Rampant weeds grow long between each, but mostly the playground is soil, red and dusty. The classrooms have doors, but the windows are just carved long rectangles, like church windows without glass, which let the breeze, when it comes, rush in and out.

The children are so well behaved. 'Yes, miss. Yes, madam.'

When we enter the back of the classroom and perch on teeny tiny chairs like strange voyeurs, they turn around with wide smiles, 'Welcome,' they say in sing-song voices.

Somewhere a bell rings, ending class. Instead of running outside they calmly stand, push chairs under desks, hold hands and walk outside. They've left their desks immaculately clean, even the pencils are lined up. What magical order has been created in a land so wild?

Outside, one straggly tree stands lopsided in the centre of the yard. When we follow them outside, games are immediately discarded, a piece of rope lays where it is thrown, food remains uneaten in small brown bags – the children gather en masse, most interested in us.

Rosie, a little girl of about six, licks the palm of her hand so it is good and sticky and slaps it into my mine. I feel the squelch of her spit bind our hands together, and part of it drips down my fingers. I look down at her wide eyes, deep brown, browner than the darkest cacao. She wriggles and yells if any other children get too close to us.

Another girl grabs my little finger on my right hand, another my thumb. My hand now taken, someone lunges for my forearm. They want to hang on to any part of my body. Ant too has a friend hanging on her arm, a small boy of about six, and a tall girl has found Tiff and clutches on for dear life. Are they starved for affection?

A little boy clambers quickly up my back like a monkey. Wrapping his arms tightly around my neck, he almost chokes me. Despite Rosie's best snarls and growls to keep me to herself, she can't fend off the insistent attempts of the other children. An older boy, about twelve, stands in front of me, feet planted solidly, large eyes like coffee cups, black in the middle, dash of cream on the outside. He's taller than most of the others; his head reaches just under my chin.

He puts his hand in mine, the one that Rosie has licked, and we squelch together what I think is going to be a handshake, but instead he uses both hands and grips my white palm in the middle.

'I'm Hunter,' he says in a soft voice.

'Kate,' I smile.

After that Hunter doesn't leave my side. Rosie soon grows tired of sharing and runs off to find another *mzungu* (white person) to claim.

'Watch Kate, just watch,' he tells me, picking up a handful of old leaves and grass from the edge of the yard.

In under a minute he has made me a grass necklace. He places it gently it into my palm and I slip it over my head. 'That's brilliant!'

He smiles for the first time, and I see his eyes twinkle and crease, and his teeth shine so brightly.

After lunch, the younger children must stay behind for extra lessons, but the older children can walk into town with us, and are allowed out until dusk.

The town is small. One main red dusty road. Makeshift carts have been set up outside every second house. Oil vats bubbling, local men with wiry arms and stained white shirts fry fish and other water creatures giving the air a scent of salt.

Women workers walk to and from the direction of the river, towels and tops neatly folded in bundles and balancing on their heads. Sometimes a baby too is balancing, swaddled into their backs, calmly sleeping or looking over their shoulders at the world around them.

A market has been set up in time for the weekend. I have not tracked the days and couldn't say if this market was just beginning or ending, but we're lured by the idea of cheap knick-knacks – whatever they may be.

Second-hand clothes falling apart, rips in the neckline, tears down the arms of shirts. To wear, or for rags to scrub house floors? Old keys. Wrangled metal that perhaps could have been coat hangers in a past life. Copper wire for heating. Ancient burners and oil vats for use at home or at the stalls. A workman covered in oil is selling pans of all sizes, charred and second-hand, they've seen the flame of many fires.

Outside little houses, women crouch over naked flames and fry in one large pan a porridgey gruel poured into patties. Stalks of corn lay near their feet.

Ant's thirsty.

'Hunter, where can we buy some water?' I ask him.

He puts up his hand to signal *Wait please*, and runs off, his little legs pumping under him. Two minutes later he's back, carrying an old plastic cup of water. Ant looks at it warily, but accepts it with grace.

Further down the road, Tiff needs a lighter.

'Hunter, do you know where we can find a lighter?'

He makes the *Wait please* signal and runs off. He opens his fist slowly to reveal a used box of half matches. What a wonderful helper! We pay him, even though he says we can take it for free.

Up the road a cheap clothes market selling more second-hand clothes spills haphazardly out of baskets. Some are torn, or ripped, or faded, but they're clean, washed well, scrubbed by the women I have seen at the edge of the lake. Beating clothes with milky suds against the rocks and then rinsing them and draping them carefully on broom handles, propped between two logs.

A group of teenagers sprawled on the ground stare as we walk past. They all wear caps, perched so high on their head I think they may fall off if they move suddenly, or at all.

'Why are their hats like that, so high?' I ask Hunter.

'They have ice in there.'

'Ice?'

Hunter makes the *Wait please* signal again. He calls out to the teenagers who are kicking rocks and looking mischievous. He beckons them over and one of them, a cocky one in jeans, his t-shirt off and slung over his shoulder, sways within inches and eyes me up and down.

'Show her,' Hunter says.

'How much?' the cocky one looks at me.

I laugh, 'I'm not paying anything, but good try.' I like his optimism.

He laughs too, 'A cigarette?'

'No.' I consider, 'How about a bracelet?' I show him a line of seashells I had bought from the markets a few towns ago.

'Definitely.' He takes off his cap. Underneath is a raggy tea towel folded in a square. He holds it in his hand and unfolds the cloth, revealing a chunk of melting ice the size of my fist.

'It helps in the heat,' he says, reaching for the bracelet.

The other teenagers gather round and they too unwrap their head scarves to show us the wonky blocks of ice that keep them cool.

We stop at a small stall. I say stall, but it's just a man sitting on a milk crate with a ratty tarpaulin on the ground displaying jewellery. Tiff and Ant pick them up and try them on. They are copper wire, melded and moulded into beautiful designs, flowers and stars. Rings of many sizes. They shine in the sun.

Hunter makes the *Wait please* signal. He runs away and ten minutes later, while we amble through the rest of the markets he stands in front of us, brandishing a long copper wire in his hand.

He grins. 'For you,' he tells me.

'A wire?'

'No, no,' he laughs, throwing his head back and gurgling as if I have just told the funniest joke.

He stares intently at the copper in his hand, twisting and turning, coiling it, sticking his tongue out in sheer concentration. He works carefully, as we stroll through town. He stays close to me, like he is my natural protector. Close enough that our arms sway against each other. He smells of salt and cooked fish; this is a seafood village. I'm so close I can see the spots where his hair grows in tight curls and clump close to his head.

We stop for a moment to watch a clutch of chickens and a rooster strut by as though they own the town. Hunter is so close his body leans into mine, like he can't hold his own weight anymore.

At the school we wave goodbye. Without saying a word, Hunter leans in and hugs me. His arms encircle my waist and mine his shoulders. He is warm and small, smaller than I first thought.

We wave to each other as our group walks back to camp. Just before we turn the corner he yells out, 'Tomorrow?'

I cup my hands and shout back, 'Yes.'

I watch him safely go into the hut he calls home. And for a moment I get a glimpse into the joy it may be to have a son.

**I DO** not come from my parents.

Another woman carried me into this world. Her. My birth mother. Although there is nothing about her to suggest that she has earned the title of mother.

When I was born in the middle of a cold Sydney winter, I spent the first thirty days of my life inside a hospital. I often wondered little things. Did I see the sun during those days? Did anyone ever pick me up as though I was theirs and press me to their chest? Did I hear a heartbeat? What damage was done that can't be reversed?

At an early age (four or five), I seemed to become preoccupied with things other children were not. I began to watch them. My family. How they moved the same way. How they shrugged and pursed their lips when thinking. How they mirrored each other in ways I could not mimic.

I did not share my dad's hushed tones or soft, gentle touch. I did not share my mother's tight-lipped resilience, my sister's intellectual stance on most things. I tried many times, but it felt foreign to laugh as they did, to smile and shrug, to keep calm, to be poised and pragmatic.

They loved me, yes, but to me, there wasn't a core that linked us together. We did not walk the same, laugh the same, look the same. We did not sing the same soul songs to the night, and I did not feel the bond that comes from the sharing of flesh and blood.

I had always convinced myself I would grow to look like them. My dark hair would turn blonde, my hazel eyes would become a startling blue like arctic water under the sun. But I did not. I grew taller and wider and thicker, and my hair deepened to a dark espresso. It had kinks and curls while theirs hung thin and straight. They were quiet and calm and peaceful, and measured. And I was busy putting on plays, dancing around my bedroom, and being shushed.

I was six when I first tried to leave home. I decided I didn't want to live in a place where I didn't belong, so I would go somewhere else. I packed my bag – one pair of shoes, a jumper, my glow worm torch, a book – and I slipped out into the evening. I left the front door ajar because I wanted them to know I was gone. I walked up the driveway thinking, *Now what?*

I walked one, two houses down. There I stood, unsure. One foot on the pathway, the other on the lip of the road. I sat for a while near Mrs Louis' driveway, my backpack still on. I was waiting, like some of us do, for someone to chase me, run me down, gather me up, cover me with kisses and love. I counted the minutes it took my parents to find me, using Mississippis to mark the seconds.

Forty Mississippis until they found me.

But they didn't run towards me with the ferocity and love I desperately desired. Instead they simply said to each other, 'Oh, thank goodness we found her.' And then to me, 'Come inside Kate, it's dark.'

Walking back into the house I remember thinking distinctly, *I do not fit here.* I am not sure if I meant my home, my life, or this earth, but I did not FIT. My parents loved me greatly, but it came from a place of calmness and quiet; a place that always felt out of reach. And for me, that was never enough.

I felt I was bound by nothing more than a name to my family; and how loose it is to be bound by only a word.

**GROWING UP,** these are the things I knew about my birth mother. She was born in New Zealand, she was 5'1", pregnant with me at 27, and liked singing, knitting and reading. She was described as mature and intelligent.

Who decided this, herself? The nurse who knew her for a few hours? *Do mature and intelligent people get pregnant and give their child away?*

There is an insistence on her sanity, her level-headedness. Apparently a love of history and horses. But we all know what happened. Between the woollen scarves she made or the medieval stories she read, when she birthed me, she turned away. She simply said, *I can't.* Or even worse, *no*, and left me to make my own way through this world.

When the law allowed it, her name was delivered to me in a crisp slim envelope from the registry. The font was faded and slightly ajar, but you would only notice this if you stared at it for too long.

Her name was Lillith. And she had named me too. Sarah.

I wondered, *Had she looked at me and thought me a Sarah?*

In Hebrew, where it originates, Sarah means princess or noblewoman. Sarai appeared in the Old Testament; she was the wife of Abraham and spelt her name with an i at the end until God later changed it to an h. Later she committed the spectacular feat of giving birth at the age of ninety to Isaac.

Kate, or as I was christened, Katherine, is decidedly more unknown in its derivations. (The irony here is not lost on me.) From the Greek Aikaterine, the etymology is debated: it could derive from the earlier Greek name Hekaterine, which came from *hekateros*, meaning each of the two; or it could be derived from the name of the goddess Hecate, variously associated with crossroads and entrance-ways, she was often depicted holding two torches, or two keys in her hand.

It could be related to Greek *aikia* (torture); or it could be from a Coptic name meaning 'my consecration of your name'. In the early Christian era it became associated with *katharos*, to mean 'pure', and the Latin spelling was changed from Katerina to Katharina to reflect this.

The name was first borne by a fourth-century saint and martyr from Alexandria called Katharina, who was tortured on a spiked wheel.

Yes, I think. That's how I feel. Tortured. Like I'm on a spiked wheel.

After receiving the envelope I slept uneasily for a week. I woke at night from heavy dreams.

I was troubled. Should I search for her? What would I find? Up ahead Hecate, the sorceress, held aloft two keys. Behind her, two pathways ran in opposing directions. Left or right. Yes or no. Light or dark. *But what if you couldn't tell which way is which?*

I began to ask for guidance and advice from the world around me. *I shall search for Lillith if the traffic light goes green in less than five seconds. If there is rain today. If I see two white birds in our camellia tree.* Each time I made it more obscure, and each time I found those items that I was looking for. It seemed the entire universe was saying *Yes*.

As I knew it would eventually, saying *Yes* found me on weekends pouring through phone books and white pages and current election records. *Lillith Samson,* I thought, repeating the name like a mantra. *Where are you?*

To say there were millions of Samsons would be an understatement. I could have joined all the lines of Samsons together and, like a ribbon, wrapped it around the world a few times over.

Finally I ended up at the New South Wales State Library. A large creamy building made of marble and pillars and sandstone, tall and structured, carved into a corner on Macquarie Street. I requested electoral rolls dating back to 1978 – so old it was stored on microfilm.

'Both New Zealand and Australia,' I asked. The librarian with kind brown eyes set me up at the old clunking machine that needed a dust. It was so large that I had to stand to go through each line – highlighted in yellow faded paper, scrawled notes in formal cursive writing.

For hours I travelled through ten years and there was nothing. No death, no marriage, no name on the electoral roll. She remained a mystery.

I burst into tears and when concerned faces gathered around me, I had to pretend it was something else. The only thing I could find to say to the kindly librarian was, 'I stepped on a pin.'

That was what it was like, the tip of the needle; small enough that no-one could see, even me. But my God, when it pierced, it hurt like hell.

When I left the State Library it was grey, almost night. The winds were shaking the trees, seeing if they could pull any of them loose. I took out my wallet and found the nearest liquor store. Inside I tossed up between whiskey and wine. One you could drink faster, but the other had more effect.

I caught the train home and looked away from a mother and daughter laughing over a crossword. I avoided staring at the teenage couple kissing on the station, not pausing for breath. An elderly couple held thin, papery hands as they helped each other off the train like a love affair that never ended. It was clear the most beautiful thing in the world was to be wanted.

I looked out from the train window onto the world – everyone seemed to be in pairs.

**RAFFA HAS** tracked and traced and whittled. He has taken care to include everything I had asked for. The entire jewellery box is covered. But he has done this using my drawings not as inspiration as I intended, but as an identical copy. The star is wonky, exactly as I have drawn it. The ocean waves are wobbly, just like my original. He is indeed the finest copycat. And his carpentry is intricate, delicate, amazing. It's just that my designs look like a child has been doodling on the box.

'What do you think, Kate?' he asks me tentatively, watching me look at each end of the box, turning it upside down and glancing carefully over each side.

'I love it.'

I take the box down to the beach. There is a perfect catch at the edge of each lid, a place where the box can be shut and locked, and you don't need to worry about it spilling open. This is a relief.

I feel glad. But then I don't. I become desperately aware there is another thought making itself known. The under thought. Beneath the layers, under the leaf litter of my mind, in the soil. The one that knows this is a box.

A box.

It is not lost on me that I have come to Africa to empty something locked inside of me, something I've held inside for years. And yet the only thing I have purchased, that has been created just for me, is a locked box.

I sit with it for a while. The ebony painted wood. Raffa has sealed it with a waxy oil. It has been left to dry in the African sun and instead of cracking, it has become voluminous, shiny like seal skin.

Carefully, I open the box, and it does so with a wooded pop! It creaks slightly – the hinges, the wood still young. With the lid fully opened, I am not dismayed to find it empty.

The lake finds me. Then retreats. Finds my toes. Retreats.

I watch an empty shell rock back and forth in the shallow tide. Something used to live in its smooth moon-coloured hallways. I lean over and without thinking, rinse it and place it in my pocket. Then, without a thought, I take it out of my pocket and put it in the box. It squeals when I open it, and creaks as it shuts.

I walk along the water's edge. The box tucked, like a child, on my hip.

Down the bend of the bay, past a small patch of grass planting itself in some dunes, I find the nub of a stick. No longer than my pointer finger, waterlogged once, the tide has smoothed the splinters, worn them back better than a sander. It is gnarled and knotted and seems to have given birth to, I count them, five more branches before it ended up in the lake. A gust of wind? A storm? It too finds a place in the box.

At the far end of the campsite, hundreds of metres past the point I am meant to stop, where the tide has gone out, I find an old rock. Pressed and round, it curls with coolness into the palm of my hand, perfect for skimming.

Shell. Twig. Rock.

I go on after that, walking across the landscape, collecting items. Filling my jewellery box with parts of the world.

Giving lost things a place to call home.

I stop. Isn't this why I had started this journey, to address how to fill things up? Or how to let things go?

I carry the box back to my room where it throbs at the bottom of my bed. As if it holds a heart, beating.

**LILLITH PREFERRED** to be called Lila. Perhaps it made her sound more exotic. That was her second statement to me when she called.

Her first: I'm your mother.

I couldn't breathe. My knees wobbled. I sat on the kitchen floor, the phone cord extending, and held the receiver to my ear. It was as if the world had emptied of all things and all people and it was only her, and me.

I was wondering if she was going to say it. Those little words. 'Sorry. I just couldn't. I wanted to, but—'

She didn't. I'm not sure if that meant something or not.

'Really glad you found me!' she exclaimed, breathing heavily into the phone.

'Yes.'

She had a New Zealand accent. A peculiar lilt. I listened carefully to the way she clipped her vowels. It should have been strange, hearing her voice for the first time, but instead hearing it was soothing. A voice from the past. As if I *remembered* it.

'Well, the private investigator did. He caught me between France and Italy. Good job I had phone reception, otherwise. Well, not to worry about that. Glad it all worked out.'

'Yes.' I couldn't find words.

She said with interest, 'You sound so Australian.'

'What else would I sound like?'

'I'm not sure,' she said, finally finding silence. 'Like me?'

She took my pause as a sign to continue talking, and she nattered away as if I were a long-lost friend, an old aunt, the neighbour from up the street. *Was I grateful for that, the chitchat?* I wasn't sure.

A Buddhist, she didn't believe in the accumulation of things. She had two suitcases and a few old coats. The rest of her belongings were sold, borrowed or rented, splayed across the world hanging in new houses.

'You don't need a house or a mortgage,' she told me, 'when the world is waiting for you to visit.'

Her favourite countries were China, Egypt and South Africa. She could speak five languages. I listened intently, but said little. I tried to fill twenty-one years in that conversation, stuffing information into the gaps of my life. Gaps that opened like the hungry mouths of baby birds, empty and wanting. Hoping her words would carry me forward. For it wasn't a sense of her that I was searching for; it was a sense of me.

She explained to me that she was made to travel. She wanted to learn Arabic and German and Mandarin.

*Me too*, I thought, *me too*.

She said, 'Let's meet,' as though she were planning a party.

She would be in Sydney in six months. Staying in Chinatown.

After a rare pause, she asked with a tight voice, 'What do you look like?'

We matched on every count – deep brown hair, cocoa eyes, full lips, arched noses, deep olive skin. She said with an easy laugh, 'You sound like me.'

And after all these years of not fitting in, it seemed with ease, that finally I did.

**I ARRIVED** in the city too early. I watched people come and go from the hotel foyer, and each time I sat a little straighter. *Is that her?*

The people behind the desk were dressed in red blazers. They answered ringing phones with muted tones of importance and rhythm. 'Thank you, madam.' 'Of course, sir.' 'Yes, a 6 am wake-up call for Room 378.'

There was an older lady at the desk and I was sure she wasn't Lillith. She had a walking cane and I didn't think a tour guide could afford to be slow when squeezing through San Marco Piazza with a tour group. Although a cane would come in handy to swat away thieves, perverts and excessively attractive women.

I walked outside. The October sun was fading, and the world was hot and dark. My watch was on time, which meant she was late. Ten minutes. An older couple stepped from the chill of the hotel and headed towards the city for dinner, her arm on him, her high heels echoing until they turned the corner.

I sat and stared at my phone, then my watch. I counted like my mum used to when I was in trouble. One, one and a half, two, two and a half ... I wonder what number I am counting to, and whether you can ever really get to the end if it's a place you're not sure you want to go. I went into the foyer again, and when the cold made my arms freeze, I went back outside.

Someone called my name. 'Kate.'

I looked up, and it was her.

She called my name again then rushed towards me. I thought we were going to shake hands. *That's what strangers do, don't they?* Instead her chubby arms engulfed my waist. Her head didn't even reach my chin. Her hair was short on top and long at the bottom, dark brown and much curlier than mine.

She had my chocolate eyes, or I had hers. Her lips were slightly thinner, her mouth circled in finely spun wrinkles like strands of fairy floss. The lines of a smoker. Her nose was more of a nub and less prominent on her face, which was shaped the same as mine. A heart. Her voice was deeper, raspier, her skin brown and tanned – just like mine.

I hesitated. *After a lifetime apart, what do you say?*

'Well let's go inside,' she said grabbing my arm and leading me into the hotel bar.

The bar, if we could call it that, was a small room with chipped ebony tables pushed together and worn pink seats like I was visiting an old lady's house. The plushness of the rouge carpet and moss-green upholstery had indeed been rich in the day it was decorated, circa 1970. Now the rouge red carpets had become tattered, absent in places, scuffed. The occasional circular stamp of a cigarette burn. White wallpaper had been breathing smoke for years, staining it the colour of hay. The once-golden brocade on the edge of the cushions had turned a faded mustard.

On these nights, hot and dark, people like to lounge outside with cold drinks and good views. They like to see and be seen, their legs holding the first colour of the summer sun under white skirts and tight dresses. Because of this, there were very few people in the tattered, cold bar. An old man sitting at a stool nursed the same beer he'd had since I'd arrived. A couple of middle-aged men stared over their rums at the city skyline, lost in thought.

She ordered a lemonade. 'I don't drink, it's bad for me,' she said, then pulled out a packet of cigarettes and asked the skinny waiter for an ashtray.

I said, 'Mineral water, please.' And noticed how my voice shook slightly with each word.

Everything about this seemed strange, eerie almost. I suppose she felt it too, because it took her ages, fiddling with her lighter, to even spark a flame.

'Want one?' she asked.

'No thanks.' I patted my bag, 'I have my own.'

'What do you smoke?'

I pulled out the pack of Marlboro Menthols.

Her eyes widened. 'Wow. I used to smoke them too.'

I nodded.

'Maybe you got that from me,' she inhaled her cigarette and blew the smoke to the ceiling.

'My last tour was a doozy,' she said. 'I was at the hospital with some of the passengers – gout, bad knees, gastro, the list goes on. They say it's a 5 am to forever job, this one, and they're not lying. This one was a much quieter bunch, thank goodness.'

She spoke rapidly using her hands – a trait I recognised until now, as only my own.

My mind went spinning and I forgot to listen as she continued talking. I thought of William Blake's lines:

*I am in you*

*And you in me.*

She called the waiter over.

'Another round?' she asked.

I nod.

I hadn't dared ask at first, but now I felt the urgency lift. It gathered in my throat and when it found more force, the courage lifted it to my mouth.

'How did it all happen? Me, I mean.' The words slipped out.

**LILLITH HAD** moved from New Zealand to Australia in 1978. There were 'places that needed exploring,' she said as she waved her hand tracing an imaginary globe.

'Everyone was doing it, even though our parents felt that they were going to have to look after their farms by themselves. Sydney was magnificent, refreshing, and fast-paced. There was always something to do, rather than count stars and sheep and all that.'

She rented a house with friends, who had also drifted over the Tasman sea from the lower New Zealand coast when their families weren't looking. It was a sizeable house in the inner west of Sydney with a great garden, and the rooms were filled with anyone who wanted to stay.

'We had rockers in leather jackets, hippie girls that gave up shoes and bras in return for hair flowers, and people with guitars who would sing as we cooked. Our house had an open door and was always full and lively, with constant chatter.'

She found a job as an administration clerk for a government department.

'I worked hard, and I was good too. I was promoted several times within a year.' She stops to re-light the next cigarette.

'Peter was my new boss. He was a cricket-loving, beer-swilling lad, you know? Typical Aussie bloke. Like Shane Warne.'

She shook her head. 'Exactly. Exactly like Shane Warne. I'd be surprised if he was still alive, all the damage to that liver.'

A Christmas party come early (September and they were cost cutting), but Lillith didn't drink. She smoked. Never drank. Peter had told her to lighten up, have a drink. Not one to be challenged, she had one drink. Then she had many.

She woke in Peter's bed, and crept out in the early dawn, before he was even awake. She claims not to remember anything else. Alcohol and time will do that; smudge the mind of its memories. Shame will cleanse it even more.

'I hadn't known. Of course, I can see it all clearly now. The extra weight. The soothing taste of vanilla ice cream. The nausea when the smell of chicken pieces frying in spitting oil lifted up to my window from the Chinese shop below. And I am embarrassed to say, for many weeks – twenty-four weeks and five days to be exact – I did not see the connection.'

Sleepless nights and morning burps took her to the Mornington Medical Centre. The doctor looked up from a green clipboard and said, 'You're pregnant.'

'I took a vow of silence. I told no-one. I wore floaty larger dresses. I complained about winter weight, though I refused to believe it – even as my stomach grew more rotund, and my breasts distended like engorged water balloons. I had stretch marks that appeared like cracks across a barren dry desert.'

She took a sip of lemonade.

'My legs grew clotted purple veins like old cottage cheese and my feet ballooned until I couldn't shove their meaty fatness into my heels.

'Then, when I couldn't hide my bloated belly as extra weight any longer, I took a leave of absence from work. My flatmates started to guess and question, and despite my silence, my off-balance waddling told them they were right.

'There were no Lamaze classes, no breathing, no nothing.'

The waiter arrived to clear our glasses. She ordered another lemonade before adding, 'This is my daughter.'

She said this as proudly as if I were the pope and she was claiming me as her own. I smiled and nodded, and took a large gulp of my drink. I wasn't sure it was a title I was ready to have.

She lit a Marlboro and blew a long smoke trail.

'And then you were there,' she said. 'Small, and pink, and yelling at the world. And I signed the papers,' she blew a ring of smoke to the ceiling. 'And I—'

It took her a few seconds to finish the sentence. After a pause she said, 'I left.'

**A FEW** hours before we leave Malawi, I slip out of the campsite and find the makeshift tent. I never tire of watching Raffa whittle. I sit for a while, the scent of grass freshly cut hanging in the air. Sweat. Earth. Fish with salt.

He is carving a hippo standing squat and proudly in black ebony. The front leg slightly bent and lifted, as though it could be about to charge, or perhaps wants to be greeted, extending his leg to politely shake hoof to hand.

I wonder what other jewellery boxes he will create for new campers, and if they too are a locket that will open the past. Perhaps they will just be what they were created for; a place to store jewels and bits and bobs.

When I tell him goodbye, he cheekily grins and extends his hand. 'Thanks for the sandals.'

Not to be outdone by Raffa, Hunter has been working on his own creation. He's waiting at the top of the driveway for me as we amble up to say goodbye at the school.

He digs around in his short pockets. I notice he is wearing the same shorts as yesterday, the same stain over the right knee. He pulls out the most perfect ring with a beautiful copper-coiled flower.

'For you,' he reaches for my hand and places it in my palm.

I put it on, holding it up like he's given me a diamond. In the middle somehow is a knot of copper wire, and then the wire is carefully folded on itself to form petals. It's more precious than any expensive stone.

I had wanted to write him a letter, so I had dug around until I found some clean white paper at the back of an old diary I hadn't scribbled my way through. At the top of the page I wrote *Dear Hunter*, but I didn't know what to say next.

*Hope you're well.*

*It's been wonderful meeting you.*

*Good luck.*

Those lines mean nothing at all, less than nothing.

Instead, I reach down into my pockets and pull out a wad of cash. I had known early on this is what I wanted to give him. He can spend it on matches. Or games. Or food. He can spend it on anything he wants. I just want him to have it.

He stares at the money like I've just given *him* a diamond.

We stand there looking at each other. My ring. His money. I don't know what to say. Sometimes, I'm extremely awkward in these situations. I'm the type to hug and run, so it looks more like a game of chase, or tip, than it does a heartfelt goodbye.

I smile. He smiles. I make the *Wait please* sign. He laughs. I begin to walk away. He raises his hand in a half wave. I turn around and shout, 'Tomorrow?'

He cups his hands and yells back, 'Yes!'

I keep walking. I'm laughing, and I can hear him laughing too.

*Don't look back*, I think. Because if I do, I'll want to stay. I know me. I'll see Hunter standing there. I'll think of his *Wait please*. The ring he made. The walk we had around town. I'll wonder what life would be like if I stay. If I teach him English. If we live in a basic hut by the water. If we become people of the lake. A family.

And it's likely I won't get on the bus. So I don't look back; sometimes it's best not to.

**THE OKAVANGO** is a large inland delta in the middle of Botswana. And we are about to set sail into the very middle of it.

We must make sure everything is watertight and zipped before we leave. The canoes (*mokoro*), are shallow, dug-out tree trunks, and it's likely we won't arrive dry. We have cases of canned food piled in the guide's canoe – bags of bread, flour and maize, tomatoes already bruised, their skin sagging and wrinkling.

Water, precious water, splashes in large tin cans, the tops tightened until they click and lock, then wrapped in wet shirts to keep them cool under the burning hot sun during our ride. There are no taps, no water vestibules, no springs where we are going. If we run out of water, we'll go thirsty.

The sun has been up for several hours when we're finally ready to push off the dank, sandy banks. Black sand. Sticks to our thongs and sandals and muddies the canoes. Dirty water soaks our shorts before we even start.

Ant takes the front seat. I like this because I get to be closest to our rafting guide and the sound of the pole brushing away the weeds, carving our way through water. He pushes off the sandy banks and for a few seconds we jerk. Clumsily. Then the hull is free. We find the depths, the *mokoro* skims the surface, we are gliding.

The delta is beautiful. Hollow reeds bend at their waist, dipping their heads underwater and taking a sip. Delicate white water lilies push blossomed flower heads along the surface, skimming. Delta frogs use these as launching pads and resting spots while searching for snacks of crickets and flies. Baby reeds, saplings, reach upwards, breaking through the soft brown membranous surface.

Ant and I sit and listen to the splash of water against our canoe, the refreshing dip as the pole emerges, the thunk as it hits underwater sand. The swell as we move silently forward. When we have enough momentum I can no longer feel the jerk and thrust, our pole-man masterfully weaves us in and out of the reeds.

Our canoe surges forward silently, the pole pushing on the bottom of the sandy banks only several feet below. If I fell out, I'd still be able to stand, the water seeping at its highest to my underarms. Instead, I close my eyes, the heat lulling me to sleep. I let my hand fall over the canoe, skimming the top of the water.

We arrive at a bay that doesn't look like it's ever been arrived at before. This is real. Jungle camping.

Guides use machetes to make a space big enough for our tents. Vines are strewn in piles by the time they finish. Sap still oozing, brushing past our legs and leaving sticky trails that won't wash off and need to be rubbed dry.

Once the tents are up we need to talk about the most important communal facility – the toilet. A large hole is dug more than six feet into the ground behind some trees. I notice that the guides put their tents up on the toilet side of the trees. There's a clear view from their tents right to our bums. This will be no problem at night, but during the day this is perturbing.

It is a balancing act not to fall into the coffin-deep hole of poo, crouching low enough that the guides do not catch a glimpse of my pale nether regions. This is why, after toilet time, I normally need a lie down.

Which is fine, as there's nothing to do here. Nothing. For most people this becomes the art of relaxing; the sweetness of doing absolutely nothing. For me, I get cabin fever. Or tent fever. We can't walk more than ten metres outside the radius of our camp without a guide because of animals. And the guides are all in their tents.

There is little food due to our new and wonderfully inept guide called Gift, a local Kenyan who watches himself in the bus reflection window whenever he speaks. To my dismay, this is often.

Gift has taken the art of packing lightly and being minimalist to the extreme. On the first afternoon of three days in the delta, we've already eaten half our food. He has also inconveniently forgotten that I am vegetarian.

'No problem,' he tells me head-deep in a plastic bag. 'I've found you food,' and waves a tomato soup packet.

**HUMIDITY LAYS** thick at night in the jungle. Perspiration bubbles on the inside of our tent like cane toads' mouth froth. Outside, fireflies light the camping ground. I hear the sounds of Gift's thickly drunken voice asking Mel back to his tent. She declines.

He asks someone else back to his tent to 'listen to some music'. *That's a strange description*, I think, *for taking one's pants off*.

I sigh and stick a jumper across my head to drown out the sounds of Gift opening another can of beer and talking about his morning ritual – selecting which shirt to wear. Thankfully this sends me to sleep.

Ant and I wake feverish and early before dawn. The tent is already a sauna. I am so hot my thighs are sticking together like I've made a batch of toffee and poured the boiling sugar between my legs, leaving it to set.

But the miracle of being in Africa: today we're off on foot to see elephants and lions and cheetah and, most importantly, leopards. Although they're often the hardest to spot. Loners who prefer the cover of trees. The intrigue makes me want to see the leopard even more.

Our trip to find animals reveals nothing. We trek for a few hours, binoculars in hand, looking for signs of lumbering elephants or the lone whip of a leopard's tail hanging from a branch.

'Better luck later,' the local guide shrugs.

That afternoon we're back on the hunt. Leopards. Or cheetahs. Or lions. Lost for things to discuss, our guide brings us close to a large sand hill almost six feet high. And for the next forty minutes, proceeds to tell us everything he knows about termites.

That night I cook with the bare ingredients we can find. Onions in oil until translucent. Spinach gently heated, then wilted. Rice stirred in a flat pan. A packet of tomato soup for flavour.

Our bellies are left empty. We take them to bed, gurgling and wanting.

**ANOTHER DAY** on the hunt. No animals.

All morning people laugh and chat and make cups of tea, but there is something that stops me from joining the group. I sit nearby on a log instead and listen to them without hearing a thing.

For lunch we share bread and an unsatisfying side – half a cup of boiled rice with some pieces of wilted spinach that look as though they've been fished from the lake.

After eating I try on normality: talking with everyone, laughing at things I'm not sure I find funny. People are talking about the weather, their last big party, the art of making a good coffee, what to wear – scarves and hats and sunglasses – before we go out walking again.

I see an interconnectedness between them. Their ends circle back to each other until they become a medley of loops and knots and there are no spare ends. They continue chatting, bonding, tightening the knots.

I look down. Each of my arms lies empty. I feel I have two ends flapping against the great skies of Africa and no-one is reaching out to grab them.

A chill sweeps through me. An eastern wind rises from the delta and pounds my lungs. Inside me, a furious wind, flailing against my ribs.

The kind of wind that slices you from the inside, silently, without anyone knowing.

In one glance, I see it all – the sourness of holding secrets. Africa, and my entire trip, crashes around me in pieces.

I am still trapped. I have blamed jobs and work, and people who told me life should be this way or that. I blamed winter, and her wild winds, and the bitter cold that seeped in my bones. How easy it is to blame something that roars and seeps and freezes and dampens. Yes, winter.

But I've been in Africa for weeks now, and surely I should be warm. I have been under the sun – baked beautifully like the crust of cake; golden brown – so you see, it mustn't be winter, it mustn't be him, poor introverted soul of seasons offering forth death and transformation.

No, it mustn't be him at all.

**I'LL TELL** you something I wanted to keep secret. I once held Jason's baby inside me.

I took a test in my bathroom when I was tired and bloated and my breasts were too sore to be bound in a bra. I looked at the white stick and saw two bold pink lines. *Jesus, Jesus.* I'd been on the pill. Never skipped a day. We'd been so careful.

He said excitedly, 'We're going to be a family.'

In his mind, he saw a future. Pushing a stroller coffee in hand, scarf wrapped around my neck, a sunny winter day. Bouncing chubby legs. Baby giggles wrapping us together, tightly.

My future had looked like plane tickets and woods and lakes that needed discovering. I was twenty-one and the idea that I was suddenly going to be responsible for someone's else's life – for the rest of mine – made me sweat. I couldn't breathe.

'I can't,' I told him.

When I made the appointment he couldn't bear it. He went away with a friend. They had too much rum and slurred to each other about life.

*Life.*

After that I left Jason and travelled through Europe and tried not to think about what our child would have looked like.

I can't help thinking that this makes me exactly like Lillith; giving away children; creating things and then leaving.

**THE AFTERNOON** seems to stretch forever. I walk from my tent to the water, to the edge of the jungle, and back again. I don't know where I'm going. I feel the urge to leave camp. To just dive into the delta and swim somewhere else. Instead I stand at the edge, barely a toe in the water, looking out.

*I don't know where I am going.*

The sun sets. It floats on the delta water for the longest time. A murmuration of birds appear in the north and they flutter in changing V and W shapes across the sky.

Streaks of lilac and indigo appear not long after, and then everything turns the shady haze of dusky smoke. Shapes and shadows begin to merge before all the light is sucked to the other side of the earth and we lie in the peaty, earthy smell of absolute darkness.

Over the river, fireflies zip across the night sky, giving our camp a yellow and green glow. The moon swallows the sky and perhaps her glow lights everything in her path. Lighting the shadows I don't want lit; the places tucked away. I am uneasy. Something's happening, but I can't reach it. *Smoke without shape.*

We pack up after dinner. Small tables, fold-up chairs. Someone has found my jewellery box underneath the crates, still carefully wrapped, from the truck. I wasn't sure how it even got out here.

'Is this yours?'

*Isn't it just*. I can't get away from it now.

While everyone sits around the fire I take the locked box to my tent, put it on the floor and stare at it. I don't bother to unwrap it because I know what lies beneath.

For as long as I can remember, I have pretended not to be me. I was told it was wrong to be wild – and found myself apologising for being the woman I was.

Too sensitive. Too wild. Too weird. Too loud. Too soft. Too dancey. Too untamed. Too strange. Too hopeful. Too hippy. Too strong. Too caring. Too real. Too honest. Too much. TOO MUCH.

I took the parts of me that threatened and I banished her, muzzled her, caged her, lest people find out that I was not good and happy and nice and neat and clean. I locked her away, but she haunted me, wailing in there, wanting out.

Why do we grind down parts of ourselves; pretend they don't exist? Shave them off. Lock them away? For what – so we can fit? But how can we ever fit if we are only half of ourselves?

And all this time, I hadn't even realised that I'd moulded myself into a shape that was no longer mine. *I had forgotten to ask myself what I wanted*. I had chosen the life others had offered and so the seed, my soul, lay ungerminated, hard.

If only I knew the best way to open the locked box, I would. But I can't risk going mad. Again.

**LILLITH FORGOT.** I can't say when I first noticed. Just after we met? Maybe months later. I wrote long, newsy emails, essays. I waited on her replies like children wait for Christmas. I fidgeted, checked and rechecked my emails, my phone.

She resurfaced eight months after we'd met. She was on tour in Cairns, could I pop up? I did, I squeezed meetings together, took a day off work and landed in the hot subtropics just before lunch on a Friday. We ate in an old Mexican eatery on a balcony opposite the brown beer river that runs through Cairns, hoping to spot a crocodile.

For two days we shared meals of beans and rice, slightly warmed in the oven, smothered in cheese. We walked through the street by the river at night and laughed at the humidity, the crazy things it did to our wavy hair. We stole midnight dips in the pool when we could.

'I'll email you,' she waved as she boarded the bus to Brisbane and I took a taxi to the airport.

She didn't.

Still, I found myself compelled to write to her. Even though I was yelling into the silence.

Her emails, when they came, all started the same.

*Kate! I have been so terrible with my communication. Argh! So busy!*

And each email, never more than three lines long, finished just the same.

*I think about you all the time. I promise to write more.*

But she didn't.

Like a climber, she left picks in me, places that tethered us. At any time she could hoist herself back into my life and, just as easily, whenever she wanted she could jump away and repel at such a speed, backwards, away from me. She kept coming in, and then out of my life, like she was hard to catch. And for some reason, that was the way she liked it.

She rarely made it to Sydney. For my twenty-eighth birthday she offered me a cruise around the harbour in the middle of Vivid Sydney – a winter festival of lights. Each part of the city glittered and flickered. An orange octopus glowed with purple tentacles; the Opera House covered in green scales and a kaleidoscope of rainbows; a gigantic pink rabbit outside the Museum of Contemporary Art.

Inside a glassed ferry we travelled in style, enjoying a three-course meal with matching wines. Over a glass of wine (her only one; she still detested drinking too much), she looked at me. 'Do you want to go to Egypt?'

She offered to smuggle me along with the rest of her tour group. 'Just pay for the flights,' she waved her hand like a wand. 'It will be brilliant!'

I booked leave at work, researched bazaars and pyramids and camels. My excitement grew. I scrolled through flights, finding the best times to go, the cheapest, the shortest journey, the longest. *Could I stop over in Dubai?*

I emailed, 'What are you going to pack? Is it hot? Can we go camel riding?'

She didn't respond. *She's busy.* I told myself. *She's probably on a plane.* I said this like it was a perfect reason to be silent.

The dates for Egypt came and went. I heard nothing. Like a magician, she had disappeared.

I didn't get angry; instead, I got really quiet. There is something disturbing about waiting for people when you know they'd rather be elsewhere.

**IN THE** morning, everyone gets up before seven. It's too hot to stay in the tents. They eat bits of toast grilled on the fire, then dress for the day. There are no showers so they flick water from the delta under their armpits, or spray powdery deodorant onto their clothes.

I stay in the tent. I say I'm sick, but I'm not.

I can't remember what it feels like to be happy – whole and happy. I can't.

I listen to them leave, looking for leopards and lions. And I hear them return, some hours later, disappointed. No animals.

A group gathers outside my tent.

*Are you okay? Do you want some Nurofen?*

I pretend to be asleep but I'm not sure my eyes close once. When they leave I lie there, wide awake, staring at the ceiling of the tent. Then the box.

Tent. Box.

Tent.

Box.

The rest of the world seems to fall behind a haze of grey clouds. Rain. The sky opens up and refuses to stop. I hear them frantically packing away lunch chairs and tables. Taking the rest of their food to someone's small tent where they continue to eat and laugh.

The wind sounds like a ghost woman haunting the earth, furiously ripping up trees, wailing and crazy and unpredictable. Torrential rain guts the camp. There are rivers instead of paths. Clouds congeal into one solid mass, as though the sun will never be let through again. It rains all afternoon. I picture it rushing quickly towards the delta, filling up, breaking the banks. I pray it lifts up our tent pins and carries us somewhere else.

*If I lay floating on the water, arms open to the grand sky above, where would it take me? Would I be swirled around like a leaf, tossed in the lashing wind and rain? Or would the undertow, that which can't be seen from above, would those currents tug at me, pull me under? If I was in that river now, where would I end up?*

The thought-web begins at once. Stickiness of gossamer, spreading out in each direction, canvassing corners of my mind long since shut. Reopening doors. Prising open locks.

*It's unravelling itself.*

The rains stop as quickly as they came. Just in time for a blood-red sunset. I smell dinner but don't come out for it. They make punch (if you can call it that), with wine that they fizzed by shaking hard before opening, lemonade and some of their leftover Zanzibar vodka with pineapple juice.

Ant stumbles into the tent still early in the night, and falls promptly asleep. She snores slightly and alcohol escapes her lips, filling the tent quickly with its scent.

I wait until I hear everyone else go into their tents, the steady breath of sleep, before I quietly unzip the tent and slip outside. At the edge of the delta, I lie on the sand in the blackness without knowing why. The cool water slinks up into my hair, finds my feet, nibbles at my toes like rats.

**JUST FOUR** months ago I was lying in a similar position. On my back. In a place that didn't belong to me either. That bed had metal straps by the side, in case they decided to restrain me. Luckily, they didn't.

I didn't put up a fight when they admitted me. I knew I belonged there. I felt like I needed to sleep for a thousand years.

Lillith had arrived just twenty-four hours earlier, in the middle of a bitter cold-snap. We met for dinner. Noodles in Chinatown. She started with apologies about not being in contact. It had been a year. I kept eating floating bits of broccoli, one piece after another, but tasted nothing.

She reached over. I thought she was going to hold my hand, and half lifted it off the table where it hovered and wobbled, but she grabbed the soy sauce instead. Tipped it across her noodles, drowned them.

Outside the night had begun to storm. I had to tighten my scarf several times around my neck because the rain came lashing at us, almost sideways. She said it was too wet for me to walk to the station. *Come up to her room for tea.*

We rode the lift in silence. She poured me peppermint; lemon ginger for her. She was only staying for two nights but already the room smelt of her – tiger balm and lavender mist.

I told her the doctors thought I'd had a stroke. Just recently. And now everywhere I looked I saw flashes. My left fingers still hadn't regained full feeling.

'Oh,' she said.

That was it. *Oh.*

'Doesn't matter,' I said, 'I'm sure I'll be fine.'

Even though I wasn't sure at all.

For a few minutes we sat, blowing cool breath on our boiling mugs. Tea and silence made her talk too. Made her want to fill the gaps.

'I was pregnant before,' she said into her cup. 'Before you.'

I looked at her. 'Oh?'

'It was an accident. *Abortion.*' She uttered the word into her tea cup. 'That's what happens,' she told me, 'when you know you're pregnant.'

I froze. Heard the words she didn't say. Heard them as though she were shouting in my face.

I couldn't breathe. I grabbed my bag. Stumbled out into the night.

*Everything I am, all the thoughts and moments in my life shouldn't exist.*

*The small brown freckle below my right eye.*

*Learning how to tie shoelaces.*

*Licking cream off a beater.*

*My first kiss.*

*Can you make something, into nothing?*

She told me this. *In passing.*

I realised with sharp awareness, like a slap, that I did not belong. I had never belonged to anyone. I shouldn't be here. In this world.

*I am an accident.*

I felt myself disappearing. On the way home in the taxi, I grabbed hold of a pair of tweezers from my bag and stabbed it into the fleshy part of my palm. The ends marked me like a bite, made my skin glow red, like a snake had struck me.

Blood was on my phone. On my clothes.

Blood smeared the kitchen counter like a child's finger painting. It smelt of copper and iron. I could taste it.

Blood dripping from my elbow. There was a puddle on the kitchen floor. Would bleach clean it?

My wrist pumped furiously.

I pressed it to my chest. A crimson crescent spread quickly through my white shirt, painting a blood moon, leeching into my favourite cotton top.

I was put in the mental ward. My tongue was soft and fuzzy. I hadn't eaten. I was still in my jeans. I remember leaking across the floor, spilling parts of me on their white linoleum, a tea towel wrapped around my arm.

There was a blur of white, monotonous voices and someone tugging at my wrist as they sewed me back together.

My lips were numb. I wanted someone to cradle me, but if they came too close I yelled.

A man down the hall kept running and shouting. He wasn't wearing shoes. Someone kept following him, tersely saying, 'Dave. Dave. Get back to bed. Put on some shoes.'

A woman was wailing and wouldn't stop.

Doors hushed opened and closed for faceless people to slip in and out with white tops and silent shoes. I laid down and let sleep take me elsewhere.

There was the light and darkness that maps day and night, but I couldn't tell the two apart. I slept most of the time. I didn't eat. Eating meant I had to sit up, and that felt like it could take all the energy in the world.

I remembered bits of me, the girl I used to be, like I was falling from the clouds in fragments.

My stitches were due to come out. I wished they were the dissolvable ones but they weren't. They were great black ties that sprouted like cats' whiskers. They needed to be clipped and threaded out the way they went in.

It didn't bother me. My wrist – red, raised and marked – was shown to a trainee nurse. She couldn't have been more than twenty-three.

She said nothing but I saw judgement etched on her face. She labelled me silently.

*I'm one of THEM. Not right in the head.*

I tried to lighten the mood. 'What do you think I can tell people? I got caught in a fork fight? I have a pet puma in my yard?'

She wouldn't look at me. Finally, she said, 'I don't think so.'

I turned my face away from her and her giant-sized tweezers and watched the blank white hospital wall instead.

When I woke, two ladies in flowery tops were staring at me over clipboards.

*Have you done this before?*

*You didn't cut vertically, did you know that? You didn't actually want to die?*

It wasn't the skin, the muscles that I wanted to cut out, it was a deeper place of secrets and shadows. I stared at the wall and said nothing.

They took their clipboards and conferred in whispers outside my door. The tall one popped her head back in. *We'll organise your paperwork and discharge you. You can go.*

They called a cab from the front desk. The driver looked at me in the rearview mirror.

'You don't seem like the type I normally pick up from here.'

I stared at him. 'What do they look like?'

'Not you.'

I looked down at my wrist and it was pink and furrowed like a worm had been burrowing beneath my skin. It wasn't long after that I left for Africa.

But that woman I had been in the bed, tied with restraints, kept gnawing at me from the inside out.

**THE NEXT** morning rises stubbornly like a moody child. Water laps at the sand. We pack and push our canoes out into the delta water, sliding easily onto the glassy surface. Early morning light shapes the top of the palm trees with an angry red; they look like they're on fire.

When we get the chance to stray into the water, I dive in. The bottom is cold, thick with waterweed. Slimy shoots pull at my ankles. Pressing hard on the lake bed in the shallows, or landing with a thud, lures the thick ooze of muddy earth to spread quickly between my toes.

Brown spotted frogs throat-thump and golden silk orb-weaver spiders spin. Tall reeds engulf my head. A dragonfly flitters an inch above the water forest.

Other campers are nervous about hippos, pythons and crocs, and do the egg beater with their legs, churning the underworld and staying close to shore.

I swim out as far as I can before the current becomes too strong, and duck behind a clump of reeds; buds of lilies. I watch the others through the narrow gaps, their movements and sound cut into slits. I see only fragments; and that is enough.

I hadn't slept; all night I thought about my wrists. Lillith. The box. The knife.

*Why does the past stick into the present like a log waiting to trip us?*

I consider ducking right under again, kicking my way to the bottom. I have the urgent need to immerse my entire self, nubs of nose and ends of toes, to stay down there for as long as breath will allow. I slide quietly under the surface, breaking it with a small ripple, finding the cool skin membrane underneath.

When Virginia Woolf wrote *To the Lighthouse*, she became enchanted by water. Perhaps Woolf was so in love with it, she just couldn't bear to leave it, and so when she crouched down in the Ouse river on a March eve, she decided it was less painful to breath it into her lungs, than it was to be back on land. She filled her coat pockets with stones and let the soft arms of the water open, taking her into a shadowy underworld embrace. Her body stayed there, kept by the water world, for another three weeks.

I lean back, floating, and let the cool water slide its fingers through my hairline. Underneath, my ears fill with water and I hear nothing but the wash of rushes. They could have been eight feet deep or eighty. A haven that keeps safe all the lives I have ever had; all the lives I ever will.

Out here, the past lies murky below the water, the future spreads out above in the sky, and I am like a chalk mark disappearing into both.

Only two months ago, in my Australian night sky, Venus was strung hard. Her pearl white glow, an incandescent fire, and Jupiter, large and kind, drew towards her, each night getting closer until they hung perfectly above the crescent moon. From earth we couldn't tell that one was infinitely larger than the other; that one was a planet of gas, the other a planet of sulfurous heat. Rather, from our place, they looked the same; as if they'd been there all along, perfectly aligned.

Even when we feel as far apart as Venus and Jupiter, perhaps, our parts don't need to be entirely separate – they can just be together for a while; in whatever way togetherness might work out.

I glide past a spider in a web. Painted golden orb legs. Spinning, spinning, forever spinning.

The smell of deep earth and cool streams. I stretch my hands wide and let my fingertips trawl and trace against the reeds. They bow slightly as we touch.

I have always visited the water when time on the ground found me irritated, agitated, out of place, despairing. Oceans mostly – the salt spray seems to cleanse away time. It undoes memories and lets them seep out of my skin, like dye into water.

I duck under quickly, and open my eyes for a second. Everything is opaque and black. A place to lay upon, a place to tread and float, a place where mystery lays beneath and even so, lifts you up.

I let the water carry me to other places in the reeds. Its whispers begin to wear down my jagged edges. Tumble me, like sea glass, to arise smooth.

When I step from the water, shivering slightly despite the hot sun, I turn around to watch the lake. The water looks as though it is glossed with navy blue and gold licks, and every now and then a swirl of black, as though a tunnel was opening and closing. A mouth.

I couldn't quite work out the balm water offered. Was it the possibility of being removed for a time from the world, to be cleansed and emptied? Or does the water offer us the chance of tide, a place to fill up?

Before we push our canoes back out, I trickle a bit of water across my legs, and it feels like a benediction.

**I WAKE** easily before sunrise. The night still lingers outside in the ashy dawn, and stars twinkle in the sky. The moon's fullness hangs low and sleepy. I pull on shorts and a singlet silently, a cotton sweater. Zip the tent behind me. Build the fire. Boil the water. Take a cup of coffee and walk to the edge of the camp; then further.

Hands rest on scratched bark trees, taut and cool before the sun begins to rise. I blow on the coffee to cool it; watch the skies turn soft coral, dusty rose then quartz pink. The sky is performing miracles, and the air is still cool from the long night. Birds start singing the day to life. Dawn cracks through the sky. Cicadas take up the harmony, humming in waves.

I make toast over the fire. Squatting over piles of ash and seared logs, holding the stick at the furthest tip so my hands don't burn. Camp starts to wake.

At first light we have eaten and washed, and are rolling up tents, dismantling chairs, screwing lids on jars and packing them in the truck. We carefully place the butter near the ice cooler, the cheese too – today is supposed to be over forty degrees. We finish quickly, before the sun has fully woken. Months on the road have made skilled campers of us all.

Below us the valley surges with heat. The sand becomes coarser, losing the muddy delta tones. Deep earth seeps up the colour of blood and settles on the top baking everything in terracotta; the colour of chipped pots.

We stop for a moment in Maun. A town on the outskirts of the Okavanga. After so many days of thick jungle, the noise of the town crescendos. Chatter. Brakes. Trucks. Music booms from speakers, blaring loudly, as if inside my ear canal. Is this what it's like to hear after days of being silent?

'Who would like to see the delta from above?' Gift asks.

I imagine ascending a very tall building, like Sydney Tower, but he's pointing to a small light airplane perched to the side of a mottled brown building marked Maun Airport. It's more than small. It's miniature. I'm surprised someone can fit in the back behind the pilot. Even Gift looks uncomfortable when four people raise their hands.

The pilot walks over and introduces himself. He's South African and, in another life, he's a model. Dark blonde hair carefully styled. Square jaw, smooth olive skin. Of course, he's wearing gladiator sunglasses as though he just stepped out of *Top Gun*.

Suddenly more of the girls want to see the delta from above.

'You can go with my buddy,' and the pilot nods over to a rather normal-looking, middle-aged man standing near another tiny plane.

They decline. 'Oh, it's okay. You go ahead,' they say, looking longingly at God pilot.

I'd like to see the delta from above, to see how the tributaries run into each other, how the inlets become coves, where they flood across the plains, how the water weaves in and out of the land like a giant green and blue tapestry. But I had my moment in the middle of the delta, swimming deep into her turbidity. Something tells me I'm ready to move on now.

As God pilot throttles down the runway and carefully lifts the steel bird into the sky, I'm sitting with the others on a dusty bench in front of a bus stop. A man is selling postcards. Aerial views of the delta. *That will do me*, I think and purchase one. That's all I need from here.

**IT GETS** sparse as we leave Maun. Huts and houses are spaced out. We pass the last few huddles and after that it's just blue skies and sandy soil. I find myself staring out the bus window, thinking about nothing. Run my hand over the carpeted truck seats, the blue plastic trim.

The others are all sleeping. Leigh is covered in a Kiwi flag. Ant is out cold as though someone has clocked her on the head and she's collapsed across the seat. After being with each other for weeks, thankfully we are wrung out of conversation and sink into the lull of contentment.

We have learnt that words do not need to cover silence.

I tilt my head and rest it on the window. Tussock grass below, flashing past our bus windows. The land forms new cracks, splitting under the sun; parched lands thirsty for a drink. Off in the distance, the horizon moves and I watch as the specks of white become zebras and water buffalo and bison swaying together.

After an hour I feel myself dozing in the heat. The truck stops. Toilet break. Everyone is tired and moving like they have no bones in their body.

When we first started in Kenya, we scrambled for large trees, to squat behind them. Toilet breaks became long stops as we clambered sometimes a hundred metres up the road looking for privacy.

'You watch, while I go,' we said to each other.

One by one we took turns squatting behind the trunk, checking each direction several times.

'Are you watching? Is anyone coming? Are we okay?' we yelled before committing to the act.

A last-minute bout of anxiety flushed us – that can happen when you're wearing pants around your ankles – but soon we realised no-one was coming. More relaxed, we found ourselves going together, thin veils of trees between us.

Of course, there was every opportunity to see someone else's bum, but out of respect, and because that could have been us in full view, we had an unspoken rule. *No looking*. Stare at the ground, watch that you've put your feet in the right place, ensure your dress or skirt or pants are hocked up at the right angle to avoid splashes, or worse – being in the path of full trickle.

There were lessons learnt – some quickly. Especially when you went near the acacia trees that dropped leaves as sharp as needles. These pen-sized spikes could pierce through rubber thongs like they were soft butter. *Don't squat too low*. More than once or twice we heard the double yelp of someone who got too close to the tough briar bushes that covered the land. One yelp when the spike went in, wedging itself deep in soft white buttock flesh, and one louder when the wounded had to reach around and pull it out.

But as we worked our way out of Botswana and towards Namibia, there were less trees, fewer tall grasses. There weren't even any briar bushes left to squat behind.

We stop on a small shoulder of the dusty, gravel road. Off in the distance there's a tree. One scraggly tree. It would barely reach my head in height and the trunk is no wider than a fence post. We may as well squat right here in the sunshine as try and find a place behind it to cover us.

Quickly we decide we can go one by one, just a few metres from the truck. A casually flung scarf, transparent in the sun, is held up for what little privacy it offers. Thankfully the roads are empty; no other buses have passed.

We climb back onto the truck and continue straight ahead. The terrain flattens even more. Small hills and bulges become tiny knee-high mounds, and then it's just flat and straight. Because we're heading due west, the sun finds us eagerly through the windows.

I feel the strength of the rays feeding my skin. Kissing our shoulders, making us ripen. I'm darker than I've been in years – since I was a child and refused to go inside during the hot, summer months. Back then, there was the constant ritual of sitting by the pool until I got too hot, then diving in, the freshness of water fizzing around my ears, instantly cooling my body. What we wouldn't do to find a skerrick of water out here. To drink. To bathe. To dive into.

My hands have dirt smudged across the palms. Where is that from? My feet wear the permanent marks of thongs – a white strip that lies like an inverted V below my toes. It could be a suntan, but it's possibly dirt too.

At home I hated the thought of being so, well, *dirty*. I'd be showering, or planning my next shower. And nothing was better than my lovely, clean shower at home. Strong and hot, I could linger in there for hours. I turned my nose up at public showers. I wanted it clean, and to have no bits of other people; stray hair strands, or the mottled gunk you find on shower floors when you share them.

It is strange how happy I am without the comforts of my life back home, and this surprises no-one more than me. I remember how I never had enough skirts, or how I snuggled in bed all weekend with a raft of books. How strange it all seems to me now. *I don't care anymore.*

I am learning how little you need to get by. No hot water, no air conditioning, no electricity. Our food is cooked over the heated coals of a fire. Everything tastes the same yet wonderful – of smoke.

Cleanliness is *not* next to godliness here. We are dry and dusty and parched and covered in sweat and dirt. Tonight we will scrub our underwear in river beds or tiny rusted camp sinks without washing powder or machines or dryers. Life is less exhausting when it is simple.

**THE SUN** is brilliant and high. We stop by a small town. Shanty houses, walls and roofs made from old pieces of tin roof, large rock bricks, the mortar made from local mud. Here in the African dust, farmers sell their produce by the side of the road.

An old man wears a torn jacket with bold letters that read *Niked*. He is quiet, alone with his thoughts, unassuming, and beautiful to watch. The deeply creased lines on his face, the greying tinges at the widow peaks of his skull. Soft padded fingers delicately separate vegetables, patting each one of them into place as though they are his children. Freshly picked, still covered in the ground they came from – oversize brown potatoes, bursting pea pods, bent carrots.

Sometimes we find apples. Pumpkins large enough to hug. Rarely oranges. Mostly there are bananas, brown, broken and soft. Picked and piled on a piece of ratty blue tarp, held to the ground at each corner by large rocks.

Someone buys bananas and hands them out on the truck and before we even open them, the ripe flesh oozes out the top, through small slits in the skin. We eat large mouthfuls of the white flesh, ripe and gooey. I glance at Ant and she has banana across her hands.

'It's delicious,' she says, licking her finger.

It's true. It tastes like cake batter.

'If we lived here,' I say, 'I'd buy bananas from that man every day.'

'Could we live here?' she asks.

Isn't that the question I've been asking all along? In Kenya and Zanzibar and Malawi and Australia and Paris and Italy – *could I live here*?

Of course. We can all live here if we want. Every place offers a certain something, a sense of excitement in offering what we don't have.

But I'm starting to realise, perhaps it isn't a country that I've been searching for. Or a city. No. Something has been unearthed out here and presented itself to me, like that postcard of the delta.

And I'm seeing it from above, my life, as if for the first time.

**ON A** map, Namibia floats at the south-western cape of Africa, a long sandy stretch that meets the Indian Ocean, and then turns back on itself and juts into the middle of the continent, stretching for miles into desert. Angola lies to the north. Botswana to the east. South Africa below.

The border crossing is lengthy. Thousands of pedestrians, cars, utes and trucks also want to make their way into Namibia today.

We're told we must disembark and walk – with our shoes on – through a tub of soapy water. Signs everywhere demand we save Namibia from foot and mouth disease. Even the truck has to be driven in a perfect line, its wheels lined up against soft squishy antiseptic pads that bubble with soap when it lumbers over them.

We wait for hours, almost three, for our passports to be stamped. We swelter in the heat. It's even hotter, if that's possible, inside the small brick hut marked with a lopsided blue sign that reads *Immigration*. Fans are on strike. There's no air conditioning. Our truck is locked and would be hotter still. So we sit outside, in the stifling heat, moving only to swat away flies under the single shadow of a baobab tree.

Back on the truck we travel through desert. Flat. Red. It's as if the earth's crust has been sliced open and her blood has seeped up, staining every grain of dust. The red of desert dirt, of Mars. Overhead stretches of blue silk sky. It's hard to imagine a place with more space.

Nature turns up the oven dial, and daily temperatures hug us in heat before the sun has even risen. Hazy days where the mercury hits forty and all you can do is sag under the weight of heat and lay still. The hot winds are fierce. Strong and dusty, they burn our faces, wrapping us in earth and sweat. The Westerly gusts scatter red dust all the way from the desert, spilling Namibia from the inside out.

Driving with the windows closed becomes unbearable, but with them open, it's like sticking our heads into a furnace. We nurse water bottles that bubble in the heat. I sit with one leg bent on my chair and the other in the aisle, some weird frog-legged position, and shove my skirt underneath each thigh, wrapping them so they don't stick. I sweat like I'm made of water and when I exit the bus at bathroom breaks I have damp, soggy patches of skirt. The wind blows me dry within minutes.

We stop for lunch. Hunks of tomato, tails of cucumber and soggy bread. It's too hot; no-one can eat. The grated strands of cheese melt on top of each other.

We're still so far inland, there are no coastal breezes or water anywhere. The last bit of water I saw was the tub of soapy suds at the border crossing and before that, I can't remember.

I love this place. But what I wouldn't do right now for a screaming cold African shower.

**SAND IS** in everything. Our clothes. Hair. I find a pile of it like a mound in my right ear. When we eat lunch it's always accompanied by the familiar crunch of sand between teeth.

Everything is red. Scolded. Scorched. Even the trees have a sugar dusting of Namibian soil. Anything white is now a dusty rose. T-shirts. Socks. Our skin.

It is terrible bus-driving weather. Matilda is burning up like a feverish child. Having the windows open doesn't make a lick of difference. Closed, it begins feels like a pressure cooker.

Scott says, 'Something has to be better than this,' and opens the window.

I feel like I'm at a hairdresser's and all of them have pointed their extra hot hair dryers at my face on the fastest speed. Our lips wobble against the air pressure like we're skydiving.

Straight roads. Red soil. Nothing else. Days pass. Each night we sink fatigued into our tents. No-one speaks. No-one drinks. The party bus has exhausted herself. We're a place of sleeping.

Our tents smell, and so do we. Showers are wonderful when we can find them. We learn to improvise. Wet tissues can soap an underarm quickly. You can get a good ten wipes in there if you're careful, before they disintegrate.

Nothing moves out here. There are no birds. No animals. When we stop on the dusty stretches for a chance to squat and pee a few, miserable dehydrated drops, there aren't even any ants. I know this, because I spend time bent over, trying to find them.

The sun continues. No clouds. No chance of rain. We are in the middle of the middle of the desert.

I'm finding it hard to move. To think. I wonder if the sun is broiling my brain. Hunter's ring is chaffing me. My fingers have swollen like fatty sausages. Every part of me feels on fire. I could spontaneously combust. And despite this, I want it all. Every bit of it.

I feel more alive out here than I ever did back there, on the train, going to work – same nights, same days. Frantically doing things, and going nowhere.

How delightful it is, to thaw out. The freeze has left and the earth is on fire. I can feel everything. The heat on my face. Every grit of sand in my teeth. The dry air in my lungs, scratchy and hard.

I look out at the stretch of barren land in front of us. I have a feeling that I'm on the edge of discovery; there is the smallest glimmer. An inkling.

*What if none of us are meant for fluorescent lights and technology and soft bellies? What if we're all meant to be under the hard, blue sky?*

'**THERE'S A** zebra's head!' comes the call when we're in the middle of Etosha National Park.

The truck radio is scratchy. A loud blast of white noise.

'Fresh kill,' the ranger's voice says again through the bad line.

Gift is gathering everyone quickly. The words, *zebra's head*, move around camp, gathering momentum, chanted like a mantra. People are gathering cameras, additional filters, zoom lenses.

Scott says, 'This could be the money shot.'

Steve wonders how close the trucks will be able to get.

*I don't want to go*, I think.

Candy is yelling at Bazz, 'Get the video camera too, honey.'

Ant is wondering if it will get cold, it's almost sundown.

*I don't want to go.*

They tumble into the truck, eager.

'Kate, are you coming?' Ant calls out.

Gift is about to lock the truck door. There's no time to wait. The lions will come back for the head soon. The cubs will have learnt how to rip meat from between the rib cage. The vultures will circle and wait for their turn. The flies have already begun to land and lay their eggs, and it will take less than a day until the entire corpse is being eaten from the inside by newly hatched maggots.

How do they know when something is dead, the vultures and flies and maggots of the world? How do they sense it? Because they do know. They can smell the unique scent of sulphur that decaying meat emits almost spontaneously upon death. They know the moment it happens. Rangers can spot a kill from miles away. The circle of vultures in the air ready to scavenge.

Would it be a good sense to have, to know when something in our lives has died?

'Kate?' Gift calls out.

Last chance.

Just weeks ago I would have said yes. I would have grabbed my camera too. Got on the truck. There would have been a sensation in my stomach, *Maybe this wasn't the best idea*. But I would have swallowed it down. Shrugged it away. I would have thought, *That is so dangerous, but everyone else is doing it and they look so happy.*

But something had seeped out of me in that delta, something has loosened its hold, let go.

*No. I don't want to see a decapitated zebra.*

'No, you go,' is all I say.

The truck door bangs shut and they rev the engine all the way down the dirt track, shifting in and out of gears as though making a getaway.

Then it is just me and the park and a few empty tents.

What a strange feeling it is, this lightness. I sit down with a book and open the front cover and read it without interruption.

The others come back full of stories of blood and gore. Talk around the dinner camp circles around the zebra head.

'I could see bone.'

'There were veins still pumping out blood.'

'The smell! It was horrid. Decaying.'

It is amazing they can eat the lump of beef broiled in brackish water for dinner.

**AFTER DARK** we walk through the camp to a lookout that we've been told is a must-see. Walking along the darkened track, the only light spilling from head torches reveals an array of trees, rocky outcrops where snakes coil in the day.

The viewpoint overlooks the Etosha pan, a vast, bare, open expanse of salt. The largest salt pan on the continent. Originally a lake, it dried up centuries ago when the Kunene River in Angola changed course, heading to the Atlantic Ocean. Over the years, the lake dried up, leaving behind an enormous salt pan over 130 kilometres long and 50 kilometres wide. In the language of the Ovambo tribe, Etosha means 'great white place'.

At night this particular place is said to be a busy location where animals gather to drink from a small watering hole. We've been told to expect giraffes, elephants, lions, warthogs, ostriches, rhinos and perhaps a leopard.

The lookout is basic. A large outcrop of rocks. Someone has built a small shelter of wood above some of them and the front is gauzed with a sheet of wire, separating us from the water pan below.

No chatter. A sign tells us. It scares the animals away. We scarcely breathe. The water lays still below. A small night light reflects off it, bright enough for us to see silhouettes, but all we can see are the trees. An hour passes. Then two. It grows desert cold and we start shivering. The rocks have left our backsides numb and I can feel pins and needles down my legs. Soon I won't be able to feel a thing.

Ant shuffles back about midnight to get her sleeping bag and a small pillow. She lies down on the rocks and tries to find a comfortable place. Candy is leaning against Bazz and he, with droopy eyes, is leaning against a rock. Both are almost asleep. My teeth chatter as the wind picks up.

Legend has it that the formation of the Etosha Pan resulted from a small village being raided; everyone was slaughtered except the women. One of the women was so upset by the death of her entire family that she cried until her tears formed a massive lake that eventually dried up and left behind a huge white pan.

At ten past one I feel like crying too. My pins and needles have become those nasty ones that really hurt. I start moving one leg, trying to get the blood flow going, but it feels rubbery and strange and when I stand up, it almost collapses right from underneath me.

*No. I don't want to sit here all night freezing. No. I don't care if I miss out on elephants and lions. Besides, who wants to see them through the veil of wire? This, us and them, delineation never feels right. I might as well be at a zoo.*

On the way back it's almost pitch black. Alone, I hear the crack and sigh of the trees and branches. This would have scared me once, but now it comforts. I hold my hand out in front of me and can barely make out the edge of my fingers and the start of the night. As if by some transcendence, we've intermingled after all these months out here.

I walk back over the rocky track, feeling the grasp of trees hit my shoulder. In some places the path is wide and sandy and in others I must navigate small crevices and turn sideways to slip through trees.

I've left my head torch back in my tent; I relied on Ant's as we moved up here. But I've learnt something out here – we don't always need light to guide our way. Sometimes we can rely purely on instinct, to know where to put our feet, which pathway to tread. Carefully, slowly, step by step I make my way back without tripping.

Back in the clearing it's dark and full of tents. I can only just make them out from the twinkling of stars unobstructed by a canopy of trees. From memory, I make my way through the camp. I feel my way along a stone wall, and when I hit the wooden posts of a small alcove, near a towering tree, I find my tent.

I tumble inside. It feels so soft and comfortable lying there on top of my sleeping bag. I leave the front of the tent slightly unzipped. I wrap my shivering body in the bag and nestle down for what remains of the night.

But sleep is impossible when you're this cold. I lay there thinking of the headless zebra and the full lion. I can't choose sides. It's impossible. I want the lion to eat, and the zebra to escape. But it doesn't work like that.

Years before I came to Africa I saw a documentary about predator and prey – gazelles and lions. Rabbits and cougars. Deer and leopards. It showed animals will always try their best to escape. To run for miles. Or jump in diagonal leaps to escape the snapping of hungry jaws. Prey will swim across a lake, or attempt to cross an ocean to avoid death. But once caught, the prey will freeze. It won't struggle. It stops. Gives up immediately. It just *knows*. Death is inevitable.

I look at the dark purple sky of Africa through the small tent window, scattered with stars. I've learned so much from being out here. To trust my instincts. To go where the water is. To avoid, if possible, losing my head. How to smell the sulphur in my life. And know when it's time to walk away.

**THE SKELETON** Coast heaves with seals and waves. Every space is taken. Penguins are on high alert, cruising the water's edge, diving through the water only when they feel safe. The sky is full of white-flecked gulls.

Seals lumber to the waves. When they find the frothy edges of the tide, they shimmy like silken dancers, graceful and sleek, riding through the rumbling waves. We get a flash of their gunmetal grey tails. A quick salute of a flipper, like they're waving.

The smell, all kinds of it, is rancid. Old fish carcass guts and small penguin poo, runny plops from passing pelicans and the fishy breath of seals. The midsummer sun comes and bakes it all like bread in the oven, the tops become crusty and hard. Gift suggests we have lunch here. Lunch. The smell hits me in the face no matter which way I turn. I am amazed that other people gulp down sausage sandwiches.

I take the time to walk to the other end of the dusty road, along the cliff side where the earth drops away suddenly, a long twenty metres to the sand below. I leave the path and push through to the very edge where a lone line of metal chain was meant to prevent people from falling over. It would do little if that is what I am planning.

*Luckily, I'm not.*

*ways to come home*

The sky is full of squawks. Birds swoop and dart and soar, seagulls and pigeons. A pelican watches from the heights of a curved light, overhead, waiting for the moment to dart down and grab a fish for lunch. I'm sure to be covered in poo soon, but I don't care. It all stinks and I might as well stink along with it.

The entire shore, from the south of Angola down through Namibia, about 16,000 kilometres in total, is called the Skeleton Coast. Shipwrecks, old and rotting. Rusted hulls. Overturned in storms. More than a thousand boats found a sudden end here, and now lie creaking and fading under the heat. Years before the sailors and their shipwrecks, this place was an animal graveyard. A bay of bleached white whale and seal bones and the men who cut and killed them for fat and fur. The future must have seemed dismal then. A cove of blood. A beach of bones.

*Have we not all felt like this at some time?*

Where it feels like nothing is moving, nothing is turning out how we wanted, how we expected. How stagnant that can be – viscous like honey, everything sticky and solid.

All I wanted was to grow light and lift into the air. But I was trapped close to the earth. I slept, and ate, and moved through my life, a ghost in the corridor; on the couch; riding the train to the city. I was a chrysalis formed tight. It was a time of lying still, being bound; not breathing. Of letting others carry me. Moving then would have been dangerous, for greater things were occurring beneath the surface.

I am transforming. Of course, now I see it. *How could I not?*

I lie down on the grass and watch the sky, gulls dropping and circling, coming out of the waves with tiny silver fish flapping in their beaks.

Sometimes it is necessary to lie there, like the bones and shipwrecks on the Skeleton Coast. And wait. *Patiently.*

And sometimes it is necessary to open your wings, take to the wind, and move.

'**YOUR LIFE** must be good,' a Namibian man tells me at the markets, sitting behind his table of ripe pineapples.

'Must it?'

'To be able to leave for so long, to take a holiday here.'

I nod.

'And why Namibia?'

'Because it's so far away.'

He laughs.

'Why do you live here?' I ask.

He looks at me and pauses before he says, 'Because that's how life was designed for me.'

Even though I didn't need it, hadn't a knife sharp enough, I buy a pineapple from him.

'Two?' he asks, smiling cheekily.

'Yes, go on,' and he gives me a bag for each.

Already the scent of tropical juice wafts when I move.

I'm about to thank him and move away, but then I turn and ask, 'Do you like selling pineapples?'

Aloud, it seems an absurd and almost obstinate question, but something in me needs to know. Was this better than sitting at a desk, in front of a screen, to earn all the money we could for the beautiful houses and cars we hurriedly bought?

He laughs.

'Of course, I enjoy it. I sit outside, I meet new people. I have enough to eat, for me, for my family. I am filled.'

That night the sun sets magnificently. Blood red fills the sky. *When is the last time I watched the entire act without moving?* I can't recall; I am always too busy making dinner, rushing home from work. In Africa, I have been too busy putting up the tent, or stoking the fire.

Now I pause and watch as the membrane of night pushes the sun below the surface. The beauty of it almost brings me to my knees. My eyes sting with tears.

*Am I laughing? Crying? Is this what it feels like to be smashed open with love and awe?*

Under the glance of stars I wash the pots, the kettle still warm from the fire. I unfold my sleeping bag in seconds – an easy routine. Tent up and standing in minutes. Could do it in my sleep.

We sip hot chocolate from a powder boiled in water over coals until our eyes droop and our happy, weary bodies call for bed.

I don't want to be inside tonight, not even under the thin cover of a tent. I want to be outside, under the stars. I want to feel the soft drift of night upon my cheeks. To watch the moon sail across the sky.

The darkness of night's embrace enfolds me. Everyone else is asleep. As I lie under the stars, I smile at the sky. My heart has never been so full. I'm beaming, too. It's more than I've ever wished for.

When I started this journey, nothing would open for me – chestnuts, doors, answers. But now, everything is opening. It feels like a spring breeze. I am filled.

**THE ROADS** have changed. They are sealed, all of them, with multiple lanes. There are billboards for radio stations and churches. There are tunnels with electric lights. Petrol stations have flashing signs and a queue backing out the driveway. Inside their fridges are switched on and they work. Lemonades are cold. Pies are hot. Children have shoes.

I slide open the truck window at the traffic lights. (I haven't seen one in months.) Next to the road two young boys are playing soccer in the dust – with a real soccer ball. One scores and takes off his shirt and hollers and whoops like he's just won the World Cup. The other one laughs loudly. I smile at them.

One waves. I wave back.

*How could I ever leave?*

The heat drives an intensity between us. We sit silently, on the edge of something, as the truck rumbles through cities and suburbs, unbroken slopes, terraced vineyards, houses with balconies.

We pass vineyards and fruit orchards, grass that shifts in the breeze, manicured hedges. Rivers run, irrigating the banks, lush and fresh. It smells of meadow.

After two more hours, we are deep in South Africa rolling towards Stellenbosch. And today we are doing something remarkably suburban. We are going wine tasting.

Girls in pretty frocks and boys in their best shorts line up to be guided through the underground cellar filled with deep vats of wine. The day is bright. Blue sky stretches like reams of silk above us.

Inside, everything smells of earthiness and fermentation. The cellar walls, deep and wet. We take many winding staircases past barrels and bottles and more barrels until it feels like we've found middle earth. Shelves and racks and lines of wine bottles. Full and stoppered, ripening.

Back into daylight, we sit by a fountain at wrought-iron tables and heavy chairs and listen as the sommelier explains the fine art of matching grapes with food. We sample cheeses – crumbly cheddars and sharp blues, feta with raspberries, creamy cheese with apricot, a sharp pecorino. The blue is a standout, the sharpness smudged perfectly with a mouthful of shiraz. With full bellies, we sit in the sun with our last tipple as the moon appears above the glow of sunset.

Africa smells of smoke. The deep wood smoke of a campfire, rubbish and tyres burning in a heap. Candles at night when the electricity won't work. Bonfires on a beach. Flames shooting to the sky. Matches struck against a box. The thin plumes of smoke from cheap hand-rolled cigarettes. The smell of smoke is gathered in every crease of my clothes.

Meanwhile, Stellenbosch smells of crisp white chardonnays (pineapple and passionfruit) and spicy gewurztraminers (sweet gardenia blooms); cheddar cheese crumbled on a white china plate. It smells of deodorant and perfume and hair-sprayed ponytails. Of cleanliness and grass cuttings. Just like Australia.

*It doesn't smell like smoke.*

We are in houses and buildings. Civilisation is so close we can reach out and touch it. I feel strange finding a clean toilet with a door. A room cool with air conditioning. A waiter wearing a black vest and a pressed white shirt.

I count the days we have left until my re-entry into life. Four. *Am I ready to go back?*

Returning must be calculated with precision. Like an astronaut's re-entry to Earth, I must know the right time to resurface.

A breeze ruffles the canopy of trees. They shiver and the sun drops slightly. Ant brings an especially lovely sauvignon blanc to the table, and in the afternoon light we toast it to the mountains. Ailie carries over more plates of cheese – nutty rinds, mushroom bries, silky camembert, vintage cheddar – and we take too many photos. The cheese goes down quickly, as does the wine.

'Did we make it all this way?' Ant says as the sun begins to set.

It casts a mellow light across the mountains opposite. Mountains that could take years to explore, to dig up, to discover. Around us, perfectly terraced hills grow grapes that will one day fill someone else's wine glass.

'Yes, we did,' I nod.

Ant holds her glass to the sky, as though expecting God to lean down with his wine and clink glasses.

'Let's drink one more glass,' says Ant.

We do. And stars begin to appear like someone is painting them perfectly, one by one, on the dome of the sky.

**AT THE** long table under South African skies, I'm sitting between Tiff and Ant, facing Bazz and Candy. Further down, Scott and Steve are passing out drinks. Tonight we're camping in our tents. I'm relieved to be away from the old, rusty springs and stained mattresses of Stellenbosch and her air-conditioned vineyards. I'm back laying my head on the mattress of the earth.

I'm eager to light a fire and boil the kettle. To shave skins off a carrot. To dice an onion for dinner. We do and eat a light vegetable soup with some old brown rolls, wrapped in foil and plunged deep into the coals until they toast. It tastes heavenly. For dessert, delectable cooked bananas in brown sugar – all the things that remind us of living in Africa these past few months.

The chatter rises. More beer and water arrives. Scott is wondering where he'll go next – Pakistan, Afghanistan, India? Candy is saying it's probably time to start a family. Ant is smiling at everyone and saying, 'I love you, possums.'

Tiff has tears in her eyes. 'I'll miss you all,' she sniffles.

There are hugs all around. And kisses. And we're all saying, 'Can you believe it's over?'

After dinner we silently glide towards the edge of the camp where a squat, stone fence separates the grass, and us, from a wide river below. We sit there, all fifteen of us, dangling our legs over the stone fence into the darkness below. The moon, large and round and full, casts a luminescent spectral light across the grassy mountain opposite. Someone points out Orion. Someone else says, 'Listen to the water.'

If I get really quiet and listen past the river, past the cows mooing somewhere in the distance, I can hear breathing. I can hear us all breathing. I can hear the noise we all sit there making. Together. No-one moving.

I glance down at the telling brown scars on my wrist and perhaps it is the moonlight, but somehow they seem to have disappeared. When everyone else scuttles into their tents for the night, I lie on my back in the soft grass and watch the sky. The Milky Way is luminescent and in between her stars, a smattering of asteroid dust as though Van Gogh has been up there for hours painting the whirling night.

The night birds begin. One coos from a tree above me and further down towards the rocks another answers him. If I stay still for long enough and concentrate hard enough, I can hear the river many hills and turns below, gurgling over rocks.

The stars unfurl like lace above. Our tent, which will be packed up and gone tomorrow, flaps in the quiet night breeze. By 10 am, maybe earlier, only the short green grass will remain. The site will return to the real guardians – the night owls, the river, the cows. And it will be as if we were never here at all.

'Are you coming to bed?' Ant asks through our open tent door, as though we're an old married couple.

Inside, she is scribbling in her diary.

'I thought you gave that up weeks ago?'

'I did, so now I have lots to cover.' She tilts her head torch up so as not to blind me as I crawl into bed. We have this routine down pat.

She puts down her pen. 'It'll be weird not sleeping in a tent.'

'I know. I never thought I'd get used to tent life, and now I'm not sure about giving it up.'

'Perhaps we'll come back.'

'Maybe,' I say as I unzip my sleeping bag all the way and toss it over my legs like a blanket.

'Maybe you could write a book about us?'

'Maybe.'

Somewhere not too far off, an owl hoots into the night.

'Can I ask you something?' she says and stops writing.

'Yes,' I say, sitting up.

'Did you find what you came here for?'

I'm silent for a minute. 'Yes. Did you?'

She flicks off her head torch. The light of night washes the tent, and the flaps open and lift with the breeze. The bird above us coos. His mate waits a beat then answers.

'Yes, and I've realised I do want to go back and do something with my degree. Finally. And I found you – my African sister.'

And we laugh.

Just like on that first night, I push aside my pillow, place my ear and cheek against the floor, and look for the cool place of the tent, where the earth has dampened. Where the wild has seeped in.

The moon finds me through the small flap in the tent window, and shines down her light. All the light in the world. Across the stream a cow moos. Further north, the elephants in Chobe park rest their trunks against each other, huddled for protection. An old Tanzanian man is picking fresh sugar bananas to sell at the morning markets. Somewhere in Nairobi another woman is arriving in the clanging city, beginning her journey.

Three months have passed and I'm here, laying against the dirt, smelling of earth. There are leaves in my hair I never want to brush out. My skin is baked by the sun – healed. It's true what they say: one life is never enough. At least not for me.

I close my eyes. Between the treetops, an owl hoots again. My heart flares, and it's all I can do, not to smile.

I'm full of light, full of moon.

www.ingramcontent.com/pod-product-compliance
Lightning Source LLC
Chambersburg PA
CBHW031101080526
44587CB00011B/778